CONTENTS

Photo Credits

Rich Clarkson And Associates: pgs, 10(c), 12(c,ll), 13(lr,ll), 14(m) 15(ll,ur), 19(ll), 20(r), 21(ul,lr), 22(llc), 23(ml,br), 25(m,ml), 26(m), 28, 29(ml,m,ur,ll), 30, 31(lr,mr), 33(ur,ml,m,lr), 34, 35(all), 40, 42, 43(all), 44, 45(all), 46, 47(ur,ml,lr), 48, 49(all), 50, 51(ur,ml,lr), 52, 53(ml,mr,lr), 54, 55(ur,m,mr,ll), 56, 57(ur,m,mr,ll), 58, 63(lr). **Allsport Photos: Allsport Rick Stewart** 2(ll), 51(mr), **Jon Ferry** 10,11, **Brian Bahr** 12(lr), 14(c), 16-17(fb), 27(ur), 20(l), 23(ml,mr), 24, 25(ur), 31(ml), 32, 37(lr) 41(ur), 54(mr), 57(ml), 59(lr), 62(fb), 63(1/2 fb), 64(all). **Vincent Laforet** 14(ul), 22(urc), 23(ur), 36. **Al Bello** 4(ul), 7(ur), 14(ur), 21(ur). **Tom Hauck** 19(lr), 18(all), 23(mr), 25(ll,mr), 26, 27(lr), 41(ml), 59(m). **Andy Lyons** 29(mr). **Stephen Dunn** 33(mr). **Aubrey Washington** 41(mr,ll), 47(ml). **Otto Greule** 47(m). **Jed Jacobsohn** 53(m,ur). **Nevin Reid** 63(ur). **SportPics: David Durochick** 13(m), 14(ll,lr), 15(m,lr), 17(c), 19(m), 31(ur), 37(ur,m). **Associated Press:** pgs, **Dave Cross** 2(ul), **Doug Mills** 4(ll), 6(ul), 7(lr), **Ed Andrieski** 4(ll), 8(ul), (lr) **Dave Martin** 5(ur), **John Gaps III** 3(ll), **Elise Amendola** 3(ur), **Mark Terrill** 6(lr), **Dave Zalubowski** 4(ul), **Amy Sancetta** 1(fb), **Wilfredo Lee** 5(lr).

Key—(fb) - Full Bleed, (l) - Left, (r) - Right, (ur)- Upper Right, (ul) - Upper Left, (m) - Middle (ml) - Middle Left, (mr) - Middle Right, (li)- Lower Left, (lr) - Lower Right, (c) - Cutout

The Gold Collectors Series™

Gold Collectors Series Sports Magazine

Michael M. Meyers .... Publisher
Mike Morris .... Managing Editor
Elliott From .... Managing Art Director
Rebecca Bruch .... Production Assistant

Contributors

KAI's Kreations, Inc. .... Layout & Design
Roland Lazenby .... Feature Writer
Clay Latimer .... Feature Writer
Ben Mutzabaugh .... Feature Writer
Allsport .... Photos
AP/Wide World .... Photos
Clarkson&Associates .... Photos
Quad/Graphics .... Printing

Publishers of Quality Magazines
H&S MEDIA™ INCORPORATED

2121 Waukegan Road, Bannockburn, IL 60015
Phone: (847) 444-4880 • Fax: (847) 444-1153

Distributed by Warner Publisher Services and ADS Publisher Services, Inc.

H&S Media, Inc.

Harvey Wasserman .... Chief Executive Officer
Stephen D. Keen .... President
Michael M. Meyers .... Executive Vice President
Richard Pinder .... Vice President Controller
Kathy Arthur .... Purchasing Coordinator
Kimberly Blair .... Production Coordinator
Jill Djuric .... Corporate Imaging Manager
Rick Kieras .... Scanner Operator
Patrick Julian .... National Advertising Director

SUPER
BOWL

80
Riddell
BRONCOS

By Roland Lazenby

SUPER!

Broncos Win Second Straight Championship

It seems that just when you think it's about to wind down after 16 long seasons in pro football, the John Elway story only gets better.

If nothing else, the outcome of Super Bowl XXXIII in Miami showed that what's good for the quarterback is even better for his Denver Broncos.

In the hype-filled days before the big event in Miami's Pro Player Stadium, a buzz coursed through National Football League circles that the 38-year-old Elway was through, that his arm had grown weak and undependable, that the Atlanta Falcons' Chris Chandler was the better quarterback in the league championship showdown.

Elway's answer to all that?

He completed 18 of 29 passes for 336 yards and one touchdown and ran 3 yards for another score, the third-highest passing yardage total in Super Bowl history, and good enough to earn Elway the unanimous selection as Super Bowl MVP.

The real numbers, though, were 34-19, the margin of Denver's victory over an Atlanta team that had never made a Super Bowl appearance.

In the aftermath, the only questions about Elway dealt with his plans for next year. Would he return for a 17th season to make a run at a third straight Super Bowl title, something no NFL team has ever accomplished.

"I'm going to take some time, relish this year," he said in the post-game din. "You got to love those challenges. We got the team; we got the nucleus here to do it. It definitely throws a kink into my thinking."

Yessiree, the Broncos do have a team that can kink your mind. If you doubt that, just ask Dan Reeves and his Atlanta Falcons. In simple language, the Dirty Birds got plucked.

"I hate that dance," Denver's Darrien Gordon said of the Dirty Bird, the end zone dance popularized by Atlanta's O.J.

Santiago and Jamal Anderson. "We just wanted to make sure they didn't have any chance to do the Dirty Bird. They can't do it if they can't score touchdowns and they didn't do that until we were way ahead."

Gordon might have done his own end zone dance with an interception return, but he allowed Atlanta's Chandler to tackle him in the open field. "My family won't let me live it down that I was tackled by Chris Chandler, and my teammates will let me have it, too. I usually take those plays for touchdowns," Gordon quipped.

In one regard, the outcome was gift-wrapped. Reeves, in an effort to stop Denver's powerful running game, kept packing eight men on the line. In other words, he made Elway beat him, and the quarterback happily obliged.

"I thought John Elway was a great quarterback when he lost three Super Bowls," said Reeves, who coached Elway for years in Denver, after the loss. "I'm sure this one put a smile on his face."

Yet it was far more than Elway. Just about every Bronco played a role in Atlanta's destruction.

Gordon intercepted two passes that set up two scores and set a Super Bowl record with 108 yards in interception returns.

Fullback Howard Griffith lowered his head and bucked his way into the end zone for a pair of 1-yard TD runs.

Terrell Davis, the NFL's all everything back and MVP, hauled the ball 25 times for 102 yards. It was his seventh straight 100-yard game in the playoffs, which broke the string of six set by former Washington Redskins great John Riggins.

Wideout Rod Smith hauled in five balls for 152 yards, including an 80-yard smoker in the second quarter that all but determined the outcome of the game.

The result of this activity left the Falcons looking as dazed as they had the night before the big game when they learned that safety and team leader Eugene Robinson had been arrested on charges of soliciting sex from an undercover police officer.

Yes, this was a Super Bowl that offered a little bit of everything. There was the soap opera of the bitter history between Atlanta coach Dan Reeves and Denver coach Mike Shanahan and Elway. There was the showdown of the league's number one rusher, Davis, vs. the league's number two rusher, Atlanta's Jamal Anderson (who finished with nearly 100 yards).

There were two outstanding offensive lines and two solid defensive units.

In the end, what it all added up to was Elway's steady brilliance and a huge bundle of Falcon miscues.

It was the kind of outcome that settled all arguments. Shanahan and Reeves had exchanged accusations of their prior conflicts during the media hype leading up to the game. But after it was over, they shook hands quickly and moved on. "He just said, 'Congratulations.' I said the same thing to him," Shanahan told reporters.

There was nothing else Reeves could say.

After all, Atlanta had nothing but opportunity. Six times they moved into scoring position in Denver territory but came away with only a pair of field goals. Those failures left them down 17-6 at halftime, a gap they couldn't close, not with Elway and Davis posing a double offensive threat. Meanwhile, with each missed opportunity the spectre of what could have been seemed to weigh heavier.

Atlanta's single highlight was the performance of rookie return man Tim Dwight, who ran a kickoff back 94-yards for a TD with 11 minutes left in the game. It was the third of three excellent returns for Dwight.

Otherwise, the Falcons had little luck with Denver's physical defense. On critical short yardage situations, the Broncos stopped Atlanta time and again. They also harried and hampered and battered Chandler into three interceptions plus a host of hurries, hits and tipped passes.

"They all hurt when you come in and lose," said Reeves when asked about coaching four losing Super Bowl teams. "I guess I'm just fortunate to be here. You go through that, and you get here, well, who knows what your chances are?"

"Coach told us that if we lost this game, it would be the ultimate loss," Falcon linebacker Jesse Tuggle said. "We worked so hard to get to this point. We just didn't respond."

"It was kind of a strange game," observed Atlanta receiver Dwight. "We established that we could move the ball. We just couldn't put six points on the board consistently."

The deadliest exchange for Atlanta came in the second quarter. The Falcons, so good in the red zone during the regular season, couldn't get the yardage on third down at Denver's eight, so Reeves called on kicker Morten Andersen, who missed a 26-yard attempt.

On the next play, Elway struck deep to Smith, who outran the Falcons' secondary. "Before the game, during the week, I took out my laptop and looked at the stats of the top receivers in the Super Bowl. It motivated me to try to get to that level," Smith told reporters afterward.

Elway also displayed a flash of youth with a rushing touchdown on a 3-yard draw play. It was his fourth career rushing touchdown in the Super Bowl.

The performance prompted a big bad celebration back in Denver, where police elected to use tear gas to disperse an unruly crowd of about 1,000 in Lower Downtown. The commotion came just after the game ended and fans vacated bars to party in the streets, where they lit bonfires and firecrackers.

For Elway, the performance highlighted a season that saw him pass some huge milestones—more than 50,000 yards passing and 300 touchdowns.

Now, the quarterback has the opportunity to lead his team to three straight titles, although before the outcome there had been much talk that 1998 would be his last season. After the

Super Bowl, reporters asked if he had thought about going out on top, as the Chicago Bulls' Michael Jordan did following the 1998 NBA Finals.

"I don't look at myself as similar to Michael Jordan. He had six championships," Elway said. "Mine doesn't compare with that situation. But I always thought it would be nice to go on top like he did, and that means win the Super Bowl."

"I would love John to come back next season," Shanahan said.

"John is the Denver Broncos and he proved it tonight," wide receiver Ed McCaffrey said. "We'll all be nudging him to stick with us."

"We'll sit down and talk about it," Elway said. "Sometimes you run out of physical ability before you run out of mental desire. If you run out of mental desire before you run out of physical attributes, then it makes it a little easier."

Asked if the current championship edition was better than last year's team, Shanahan paused. "Are we better? I really don't know," the coach said. "It's so hard to judge. Over the past two years, everybody believed. The more pressure we had on this football team, the more they stepped up. That's what wins championships."

Roland Lazenby is the author of "Blood On The Horns, The Long Strange Ride of Michael Jordan's Chicago Bulls."

"The more pressure we had on this football team, the more they stepped up. That's what wins championships."

	1ST	2ND	3RD	4TH	FINAL
DENVER	7	10	0	17	**34**
ATLANTA	3	3	0	13	**19**

SCORING SUMMARY

1ST QUARTER

ATL–FG MORTEN ANDERSEN 32 YD, 5:25. ATLANTA 3-0
DEN–TD HOWARD GRIFFITH 1 YD RUN (JASON ELAM KICK),11:05. DENVER 7-3

2ND QUARTER

DEN–FG JASON ELAM 26 YD, 5:43. DENVER 10-3
DEN–TD ROD SMITH 80 YD PASS FROM JOHN ELWAY (JASON ELAM KICK), 10:06. DENVER 17-3
ATL–FG MORTEN ANDERSEN 28 YD, 12:35. DENVER 17-6

3RD QUARTER

NONE

4TH QUARTER

DEN–TD HOWARD GRIFFITH 1 YD RUN (JASON ELAM KICK), 0:04. DENVER 24-6
DEN–TD JOHN ELWAY 3 YD RUN (JASON ELAM KICK), 3:40. DENVER 31-6
ATL–TD TIM DWIGHT 94 YD KICKOFF RETURN (MORTEN ANDERSEN KICK), 3:59. DENVER 31-13
DEN–FG JASON ELAM 35 YD, 7:52. DENVER 34-13
ATL–TD TERANCE MATHIS 3 YD PASS FROM CHRIS CHANDLER (TWO-POINT CONVERSION FAILED), 12:56. DENVER 34-19

	DENVER	ATLANTA
FIRST DOWNS	22	21
Rushing	8	8
Passing	14	12
Penalty	0	1
3RD-DOWN EFFICIENCY	6-13	5-11
4TH-DOWN EFFICIENCY	0-1	1-2
TOTAL NET YARDS	457	337
Total plays	65	60
Average gain	7.0	5.6
NET YARDS RUSHING	121	131
Rushes	36	23
Average per rush	3.4	5.7
NET YARDS PASSING	336	206
Completed-attempted	18-29	19-35
Yards per pass	11.6	5.6
Sacked-yards lost	0-0	2-13
Had intercepted	1	3
PUNTS-AVERAGE	1-35.0	1-39.0
RETURN YARDAGE	180	228
Punts-returns	0-0	0-0
Kickoffs-returns	3-44	7-227
Interceptions-returns	3-136	1-1
PENALTIES-YARDS	4-61	0-0
FUMBLES-LOST	0-0	1-1
TIME OF POSSESSION	31:23	28:37

INDIVIDUAL STATISTICS

RUSHING:

Denver-Terrell Davis 25-102, Howard Griffith 4-9, Derek Loville 2-8, John Elway 3-2, Rod Smith 1-1, Bubby Brister 1-minus 1.
Atlanta-Jamal Anderson 18-96, Chris Chandler 4-30, Tim Dwight 1-5.

PASSING:

Denver- John Elway 18-29 for 336 yards, 1 INT, 1 TD.
Atlanta-Chris Chandler 19-35 for 219 yards, 3 INT, 1 TD.

RECEIVING:

Denver-Rod Smith 5-152, Ed Mccaffrey 5-72, Byron Chamberlain 3-29, Terrell Davis 2-50, Shannon Sharpe 2-26, Howard Griffith 1-7.
Atlanta-Terance Mathis 7-85, Tony Martin 5-79, Jamal Anderson 3-16, Ronnie Harris 2-21, O.J. Santiago 1-13, Brian Kozlowski 1-5.

Attendance: 74,803
Time of Game: 3:18

1998-99 Broncos Roster

No.	Name	Pos.	Height	Weight	Birthdate	Exp.	College
83	Armour, Justin	WR	6-4	210	1/1/73	4	Stanford
27	Atwater, Steve	DB	6-3	220	10/28/66	10	Arkansas
79	Banks, Chris	G	6-1	300	4/4/73	1	Kansas
34	Braxton, Tyrone	DB	5-11	190	12/17/64	12	North Dakota State
6	Brister, Bubby	QB	6-3	205	8/15/62	12	Northeast Louisiana
73	Brown, Cyron	DE	6-5	265	6/28/75	R	Western Illinois
26	Brown, Eric	DB	6-0	210	3/20/75	R	Mississippi State
56	Burns, Keith	LB	6-2	245	5/16/72	5	Oklahoma State
59	Cadrez, Glenn	LB	6-3	240	1/2/70	7	Houston
89	Carswell, Dwayne	TE	6-3	260	1/18/72	4	Liberty
86	Chamberlain, Byron	TE	6-1	242	10/17/71	3	Wayne State (Neb.)
48	Coghill, George	DB	6-0	210	3/30/70	2	Wake Forest
39	Crockett, Ray	DB	5-10	185	1/5/67	10	Baylor
30	Davis, Terrell	RB	5-11	210	10/28/72	4	Georgia
63	Diaz-Infante, David	G	6-3	295	3/31/64	3	San Jose State
1	Elam, Jason	K	5-11	200	3/8/70	6	Hawaii
7	Elway, John	QB	6-3	215	6/28/60	16	Stanford
21	Gordon, Darrien	DB	5-11	190	11/14/70	6	Stanford
85	Green, Willie	WR	6-4	195	4/2/66	9	Mississippi
14	Griese, Brian	QB	6-3	215	3/18/75	R	Michigan
29	Griffith, Howard	RB	6-0	230	11/17/67	6	Illinois
96	Hasselbach, Harald	DE	6-6	285	9/22/67	5	Washington
22	Hebron, Vaughn	RB	5-8	192	10/7/70	6	Virginia Tech
20	James, Tory	DB	6-1	195	5/18/73	3	Louisiana State
25	Johnson, Darrius	DB	5-9	185	9/17/72	3	Oklahoma
60	Jones, K.C.	C	6-1	275	3/28/74	2	Miami (Fla.)
77	Jones, Tony	T	6-5	290	5/24/66	11	Western Carolina
99	Joyner, Seth	LB	6-2	245	11/18/64	13	Texas-El Paso
78	Lepsis, Matt	T	6-4	290	1/13/74	2	Colorado
8	Lewis, Jeff	QB	6-2	211	4/17/73	3	Northern Arizona
97	Lodish, Mike	NT	6-3	270	8/11/67	9	UCLA
31	Loville, Derek	RB	5-10	210	7/4/68	8	Oregon
37	Lynn, Anthony	RB	6-3	230	12/21/68	5	Texas Tech
87	McCaffrey, Ed	WR	6-5	215	8/17/68	8	Stanford
51	Mobley, John	LB	6-1	236	10/10/73	3	Kutztown
66	Nalen, Tom	C	6-2	286	5/13/71	5	Boston College
82	Nash, Marcus	WR	6-3	195	2/1/76	R	Tennessee
62	Neil, Dan	G	6-2	281	10/21/73	2	Texas
28	Paul, Tito	DB	6-0	195	5/24/72	4	Ohio State
93	Pryce, Trevor	DT	6-5	295	8/3/75	2	Clemson
53	Romanowski, Bill	LB	6-4	245	4/2/66	11	Boston College
16	Rouen, Tom	P	6-3	225	6/9/68	6	Colorado
58	Russ, Steve	LB	6-4	245	9/16/72	2	Air Force
69	Schlereth, Mark	G	6-3	287	1/25/66	10	Idaho
84	Sharpe, Shannon	TE	6-2	230	6/26/68	9	Savannah State
42	Smith, Detron	RB	5-9	231	2/25/74	3	Texas A&M
90	Smith, Neil	DE	6-4	270	4/10/66	11	Nebraska
80	Smith, Rod	WR	6-0	200	5/15/70	4	Missouri Southern State
74	Swayne, Harry	T	6-5	293	2/2/65	12	Rutgers
98	Tanuvasa, Maa	DE	6-2	270	11/6/70	4	Hawaii
70	Teague, Trey	T	6-5	285	12/27/74	R	Tennessee
94	Traylor, Keith	DT	6-2	304	9/3/69	7	Central Oklahoma
95	Washington, Marvin	DE	6-6	275	10/22/65	10	Idaho
54	Wayne, Nate	LB	6-0	230	1/12/75	R	Mississippi
91	Williams, Alfred	DE	6-6	265	11/6/68	8	Colorado

ELWAY

Victory Lap

John Elway enjoys one of his finest hours

By Clay Latimer

After John Elway's final home game, Denver fans gave him the ultimate Mile High Salute. They serenaded their 38-year-old hero with deafening chants of "El-Way, El-Way" as he took a victory lap in Mile High Stadium. They fought back tears when Elway told them, "I love you." They stomped their approval when he raised the AFC Championship trophy. And they remembered.

Twenty-five years ago, Denver had a sportscaster named Starr, a weatherman named Stormy, and the National Western Stock Show was show-stopping news. Now, thanks in large part to Elway, the city has franchises in all four major professional sports and a reputation as one of America's cutting-edge sports cities.

In fact, Elway and Denver are inseparable, linked for good like Johnny Unitas and Baltimore, Joe Namath and New York, Roger Staubach and Dallas, Terry Bradshaw and Pittsburgh. No one in Denver will ever forget the good times, including the Broncos' 23-10 win over the New York Jets on Jan. 17, 1999, which Elway all but guaranteed was his Mile High swan song. But there were plenty of bad times as well, including Elway's controversial refusal to play for the Baltimore Colts, three humiliating Super Bowl defeats, the withering burden of his long-time feud with ex-coach Dan Reeves, and the Sundays when he was overcome by his own ruthless perfectionism.

In fact, Elway's career has as many peaks and valleys as the Rocky Mountains, including:

- After a press conference announcing his signing, Elway turns to a Broncos official and says, "Well, I'm glad this press stuff is all done with." But the media bazaar is only beginning for the naïve rookie. On his first day of training camp, he discovers 53 reporters, columnists, cameramen, etc., studying his every move. Nearly 30 reporters stay in an adjacent Greeley dorm. One reporter writes Elway ate peas and fried chicken for lunch; another green beans and fried chicken. They argue over who was accurate.
- In Game Two of his NFL career, Elway is humiliated in Baltimore by the Colts and their embittered fans, who are still irate about his refusal to play in that city. "I want to see him killed," a female fan says. After completing nine of 11 passes for only 111 yards, and getting yanked for Steve DeBerg, fans throw garbage at Elway as he heads for the showers. Some vault to the field, where police apprehend them before they can reach The Traitor. "I don't think anybody has ever had a situation like that," said Atlanta coach Dan Reeves, who coached the Broncos from 1981-92. In Denver, many begin to wonder about Elway, and Reeves' ability to develop his talents.

"John looked so good in pre-season that I really felt he was ready and would have no problems and we would get better as the season went along," Reeves said. "The biggest mistake was not realizing how much difference there was between pre-season and regular season. I misjudged and really could have damaged him but he was such a strong confident person that ... he overcame poor coaching."

Added Elway's father, Jack: "There were times he wondered if he was going to be able to play (in the NFL). There were times when his patience got worn out. As a parent you worry about all the pressure he was under. His mother did."

The rematch at Mile High Stadium is just as discouraging for Elway – for three quarters. Entering the fourth period, the Broncos trail 19-0. But in 10 minutes, Elway retaliates against – everything. On third and 10 on Baltimore's 21, he throws a touchdown pass to Clint Sampson. On third and four on the Baltimore 26, Elway throws a touchdown pass to Jesse Myles.

The Broncos have the ball on their own 25 with three minutes remaining. Although the Colts are blitzing en masse, Elway moves his team to Baltimore's 26 with a little under a minute remaining. On fourth down, the rookie hits Gerald Willhite for the winning score. Comeback No. 1 was in the books. "People forget that comeback, but it was one of his most amazing

Victory Lap

John Elway enjoys one of his finest hours

ones," Reeves said.

• In 1986, Elway throws five interceptions against the Kansas City Chiefs, and Janet Elway, pregnant at the time, will never forget it. "There was this guy sitting right behind me, who wouldn't shut up," she recalled several years ago. "Finally, he yelled, 'Hey Elway, you can get your wife pregnant but you can't complete a so-and-so pass.' I turned around and slapped him across the face. He was pretty shocked and I wasn't very proud of myself for doing it but..."

• In the 1986 AFC Championship game in Cleveland, Elway leads the Broncos to a remarkable victory with The Drive. In Denver, the game attracts what is believed to be the largest share ever measured to that time by AC Nielsen and Co. – a 61 rating and 89 share.

During the last hour of Denver's 23-20 victory, the game attracts a 65-rating/90 share. In other words, 90 percent of the TV sets in Denver were tuned to the game. "I've never heard of a 90 share in a local market," a Nielsen spokesman says.

• In 1989, Elway, tired of being the star in a one-horse town complains to a Sports Illustrated writer about relentless media coverage and public pressure. "I'm about to suffocate ... They talk about my hair, they talk about my teeth, they talk about how much I tip, how much I drink, how I'm playing, when I'll talk to the medial. I'm sick of it. "I don't want to sound like a cry-baby, so I don't talk about it. But it's just gotten to be too much lately. I'm just torn up inside now."

Elway vows to spend more time at a home he's recently purchased in Palm Springs.

• Nevertheless, Elway rallies the team for another Super Bowl run. But after two humbling defeats in the Big Game, Broncos fans fear the worst. Before the AFC title game, a TV station asks viewers: Do you want the Broncos to go to Super Bowl XXIV. They vote 1500 to 1300 to stay home. A headline reads: "Denverites fear shame – again; Dread of loss dilutes hopes of fame, glory." "Why don't those people go hide in closets," Elway counters.

"I didn't think 31 was old, but now I'm really starting to feel old with the talk of passing the torch," Elway says.

But the 49ers humiliate Elway, triggering a new round of criticism about his game. An hour after the 55-10 loss, Elway and Janet stroll hand-in-hand in the Superdome. John turns to pressing reporters and says, "Can't you guys let a guy sulk in peace."

• In a 1991 AFC Divisional playoff game against Houston, the Oilers' Greg Montgomery punts to the Denver two-yard line. With 2:07 left and no timeouts remaining, Elway finds himself in the same predicament as the Drive. "I remember running onto the field and saying, 'Well, we're going to see if that first one was a fluke or not," Elway says. After driving the Broncos deep into Houston territory, David Treadwell's 28-yard field goal lifts Denver to a 26-24 win. The roar of the Mile High crowd moves through Denver like a tremor.

"The one thing we really had going for us in the 80s was home-field advantage"

Elway said.

• In 1991, Elway also buys a Mazda dealership with owner Pat Bowlen and Rod Buscher, the only car man in the trio. Four months later, Elway and Buscher make the largest buyout in the state's automobile history when they add three more dealerships. Elway bombards the airwaves with commercials: It's all Elway, all the time.

• Instead of drafting Tennessee wide receiver Carl Pickens in 1992, Reeves chooses UCLA quarterback Tommy Maddox with the first pick. Reeves publicly discusses the post-Elway era for the first time. "I didn't think 31 was old, but now I'm really starting to feel old with the talk of passing the torch," Elway says. Reeves also fires Shanahan, who is not only Elway's confidante and long-time friend, but his link to the passing game as well. Elway fears he's lost any hope for the Hall-of-Fame. The Elway-Reeves situation is becoming a chronic concern of fans. After the 1992 season, Broncos owner Pat Bowlen fires Reeves. Thousands of fans vent their fury at Elway, whom they suspect of engineering the move. Chicago Bears coach Mike Ditka singles out Elway for condemnation – and culpability. "(Bowlen's) letting the inmates run the asylum," he says. "I don't think John Elway became John Elway for any other reason than Dan Reeves was the head coach."

• Entering the 1994 season, the Broncos have sold out every non-strike game since 1970. They have the best home record since 1977. But the Raiders run over them 48-16 at Mile High Stadium. Fans boil-over with anger, then apathy. "The one thing we really had going for us in the 80s was home-field advantage. We lost it in the Raiders' game," Elway says.

• After an 8-8 finish in 1995, Shanahan's first season, the team is losing its hold on the city. The Broncos haven't made the playoffs in two seasons, haven't hosted a playoff game since 1991, have a .500 record for the decade and are playing catch-up in a city they once owned. The original Broncos fans are now part of a graying generation; the average age of a season ticket-holder is 55. Meanwhile, the charming, fan-friendly Colorado Rockies own a huge chunk of the market, the Colorado Avalanche own the Stanley Cup, Coors Field is the hip place to be, and the Nuggets and Avalanche are proceeding with plans to build a state-of-the-art arena to increase revenue flow and the flow of fans who increasingly flock to the NBA and NHL.

Bowlen is growing increasingly desperate in his bid to build a new stadium for the Broncos.

• Elway presses on. In September 1996, he plays in his 192nd game for the Broncos, breaking the franchise record set by linebacker Tom Jackson from 1973-86. "He was the one ingredient that hasn't changed around here," said wide receiver Justin Armour, who played high school ball in Manitou Springs. "He was here before Highlands Ranch. It even seems like he has a Western accent."

• After Denver's shocking 1997 playoff loss to Jacksonville, Elway runs off the field with a zombie-like stare, which mirrors the look of thousands of fans. It appears Elway and Bronco fans will never climb the big peak.

• On third and goal at the 12 in Super Bowl XXXII, Elway drops back to pass, sees Reggie White rushing at him from his left end spot, steps up into the pocket, sees an opening, and then wills himself 10 years younger. First he dodges a tackler, then, as three Green Bay Packers converge, Elway launches himself into a headlong dive for the chalk line. A mid-air collision flips him around, but he crash lands in first-down territory. Broncos' fans go nuts.

The Broncos, galvanized by Elway's boldness, go on to defeat Green Bay 31-24.

After his ultimate win, Elway's friends expected to find him at the ultimate bash, but find something entirely different.

"When we were driving to the Super Bowl, we were expecting that it was going to be some wild, all-nighter of a party," Vince Sakowski, a close friend and classmate of Elway at Stanford, told the South Florida Sun Sentinel. "We were downstairs at the party and it was crazy. We couldn't even get in. We called John's room from a car phone and he sent some security down for us. We had this vision of what was going to happen and then it was so different."

Elway and his family were sitting quietly among 30 friends and family members. "It was an amazing state of peace," Sakowski said. "He just sat there with all this calm. There was a nice shaking of hands and we hung out for a few hours. I hear him now talking about a weight being lifted off his back and I see it. It was the attainment of a lifelong goal a lot of people never thought would happen. Not having to answer all the questions, all the (problems) you go through, all the tests. He found out that the taste of victory is one of peace – it was almost like a surreal experience." •

Victory Lap

John Elway enjoys one of his finest hours

“"When it's all said and done and I hang up my cleats for the last time, I'd like to think that I'm the greatest back to play the game.”

Terrell Davis

2,000

Terrell Davis is just fourth runner in history to reach elite milestone

By Clay Latimer

On the sideline, running backs coach Bobby Turner held up seven fingers – signaling the number of yards Terrell Davis needed to step into NFL history.

In Mile High Stadium, the 230th consecutive sellout crowd stomped and banged in anticipation of the moment, sending a tremor through the stands.

On the field, Denver's offensive line prepared to tear another hole in Seattle's front line.

Was there any doubt on Dec. 27 – the final day of the 1998 regular season – that Davis would become the fourth runner in NFL history to rush for 2,000 yards in a single season?

Was there any doubt after five games, 10 games, 13 games?

In his rush to fame, everything invariably falls Davis' way, which is why the 2,000 barrier fell as well, on a 15-yard run that rocked the Rockies.

"I'm elated,'" said Davis, who finished with 178 yards for the day and 2,008 for the season, enabling him to join Eric Dickerson (2,105), Barry Sanders (2,053) and O.J. Simpson (2,003) in football's ultimate club. "It's almost like winning a Super Bowl."

The Davis Files have become part of '90s football lore. The soft-spoken Georgia graduate was the 196th player and 21st back selected in the 1995 draft, but he was Denver's starter by late August. He became the lowest-drafted rookie ever to run for 1,000 yards against Jacksonville in Week 13. He finished with 1,117 yards and seven touchdowns. Although he was sidelined for parts of two games because of migraines, Davis ran for a franchise-record 1,538 yards in his second year and lost the NFL rushing title by just 15 yards.

In '97, Davis made it to the mountaintop. After breaking his team record with 1,750 yards, he added 581 more in four postseason games. He also scored eight touchdowns in the playoffs, a NFL record. He capped it off by rushing for 157 yards and a record three TDs en route to MVP honors in Denver's 31-24 win over the Green Bay Packers in Super Bowl XXXII.

Coming into the '98 season, Davis held or shared 47 team records. In the Broncos' first six games, while singlehandedly outrushing 28 of the league's 29 other teams (Dallas is the exception), he added four more to his total.

In '98 Davis also:

• Became one of three backs in NFL history to reach 1,000 yards rushing in seven games. Jim Brown did it in 1958, O.J. Simpson in 1975.
• Became the fourth-fastest player, in games (50), to reach 5,000 yards rushing in his career.
• Joined Brown and Barry Sanders as the only running backs in NFL history to average more than 100 yards per game rushing in his career.

"Every time I turn around someone is bringing me some new record," Davis said.

Added Dallas' Emmitt Smith: "Has anybody figured it out yet? You gotta shut this man down. I know there's a reason to be afraid of Elway. But Davis is the one killing you."

Critics suggest that Davis' success stems from his spectacular surrounding cast, as well as coach Mike Shanahan's peerless game planning and often flawless offense.

"That doesn't bug me," Davis counters. "I'm the first to tell you that. I mean, you're only as good as the people around you. People say that a lot about running backs: 'It's the team – it's the line.' We do have a nice system. We have a team and offense where

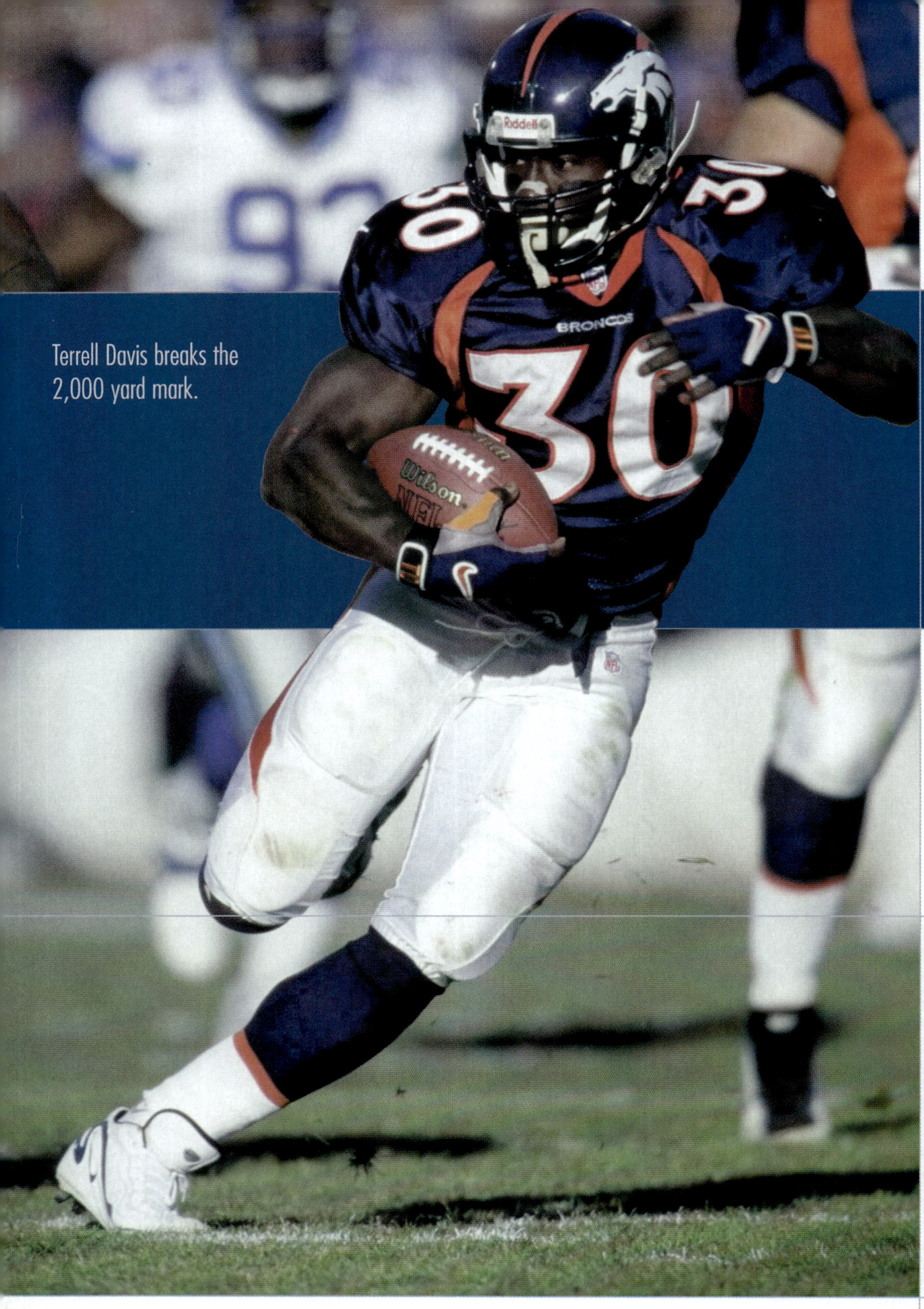

Terrell Davis breaks the 2,000 yard mark.

Mike Shanahan is a genius. He puts us in a great situation."

Nonetheless, Davis is a rare runner. He has youth, size, quickness, power, and a low center of gravity. In '98, Davis also mastered the art of reading blocks. During his Saturday downtime, he studies linebackers' tendencies, which makes his instinctive footwork even more deadly.

"He sets up his blocking better than anyone in football," said Hall-of-Fame bound Marcus Allen.

"He's the only guy I've ever been around who doesn't have a weakness," Shanahan said.

Sanders is just as high on Davis' game. "Defenses know I'm not going to run through them. But Terrell can run over you, and he can run around you," he said.

Davis peaks in the fourth quarter, when defenders sag, as well as in post-season, like Smith, his role model.

"Every time he goes to the Super Bowl, it seems like the Cowboys hang their hat on Emmitt – and he always got the team started," Davis said. "They ran the ball, ran the ball, ran the ball. I'm studying Emmitt's career carefully because I think mine is kind of parallel with his. I look at where he was in his fourth year and hopefully I can win more championships like him.

"People love winners. If you win championships, you're going to be considered one of the best players ever. If Thurman Thomas won one Super Bowl, he would be mentioned as the greatest back of all time. He wins two; there's no

"This is a special team. I know how lucky I am."
Terrell Davis

question about it. If he wins four, there is NO question about it.

"When it comes to championships, the coaches know, the players know, and my teammates know I'm ready for the call. I've never had the responsibility of having to carry the offense, and that's something I welcome. I love when

2,000

Terrell Davis is just fourth runner in history to reach elite milestone

people tell me that the game is in my corner, when they say, 'Here, we're going to give you the ball, and you run with it.' I feel very comfortable in that situation – very comfortable."

Davis is trying to become comfortable with fame. After the Broncos' Super Bowl XXXII victory, Davis appeared with Jay Leno and David

Letterman, exchanged salutes with President Clinton and signed a $56 million contract extension. He also published his autobiography, established a foundation for underprivileged youth in Denver and San Diego, and appeared on one of the 30th anniversary shows for Sesame Street.

“”One thing people don't teach you in college or high school is how to handle success," Davis said. "There's no course. That's messed up. You have success and fame and people expect you to change. But basically, it's impossible not to change. With me, I try to stay grounded, stay with the same friends I had before, the people who were there before all this happened. I don't have a lot of loose ends hanging around me."

On the surface at least, Davis appears to have successfully handled his celebrity. He still wears beat-up jeans and wouldn't think of adorning himself with glitzy chains and golden earrings. A couple years ago, he took the subway to the ESPY Awards because that's what the Average Joe does. Last year, Davis was staying at The Plaza Hotel in New York, preparing for an appearance the next morning on Regis and Kathie Lee. When Broncos media director Jim Saccomano called him from Denver at 6:30 Eastern Time, Davis was preparing to go to bed.

"He could've been the toast of the town, the limo, and the whole bit. But he said, Jim, I'm tired," Saccomano said. "He is very, very mature."

Added Davis: "I've been able to keep an even keel and keep everything in perspective because I was shaped and formed by the time everything happened. I know all about highs and lows, and I try to guard against the lows. Nothing on a football field could ever equal the lows I've ever been through."

In fact, Davis has seen more than his share of bleak times, including:

• Eighteen years ago, Terrell's father, Joe, came home, awakened four of his sons, then made them stand against a bedroom wall. To see how "tough" they were, he took out a .38, aimed, and then fired a bullet over each son's head. The boys could feel the "whoosh" of the bullets.

• A while later, Terrell's father and his mother's cousin got involved in a fight with a friend. The friend left, picked up a shotgun at his house, then returned to Terrell's house and started firing. Terrell's father and Kateree's cousin returned the fire. Terrell slept through the entire scene

2,000

Terrell Davis is just fourth runner in history to reach elite milestone

in a nearby bedroom before being awakened by a policeman's flashlight. He was nine.

• Beginning at age 7, Terrell was tormented by periodic migraines, which totally incapacitated him and even pushed him to the brink of suicide. "I'd rather be dead," he would tell himself. "I don't want to live. I can't stand the pain."

• In 1991 his brother, Bobby, was charged with murder after shooting a woman in the chest during a robbery attempt. The woman wasn't killed, but a five-month-old baby she was carrying died. Bobby was found guilty of the murder of a fetus in a landmark case that changed California law.

• At Georgia, he became coach Ray Goff's scapegoat during a nightmarish senior season that made him wonder if he'd even have a NFL career. "It's no secret I didn't like him and he didn't like me. It was a sour situation. It still (fuels) me, and maybe it needs to. That's probably the one thing that keeps me going. I feel good when I'm doing well, and he's probably watching – so that's good."

But the most radical event in Davis' life – the one that formed his view of life – occurred in 1987, when Terrell was 14. His father died of lupus, an autoimmune disease, and Terrell realized that he needed to harden himself to life.

"When my father passed away, I starting telling myself: 'Expect the unexpected,'" Davis said. "The (death) made me the type of person who kind of stepped away from people, where I really didn't show a lot of feelings. It seemed like you get hurt every time you extend yourself. As soon as you like one thing, it's gone. I realized there are a lot of people out there who can hurt you, but that you can never hurt yourself."

Davis' best years may yet come. In high school, he played several positions, and he didn't become a full-time running back in college. So his legs are relatively "fresh." Although he runs the ball as many as 35 times on Sundays, the Broncos "hit" only one practice per week, which minimizes the bumps and bruises.

And Davis is compulsive when it comes to training.

"His physical preparation is second to none," Broncos offensive coordinator Gary Kubiak said.

Davis' mental preparation is second to none, too. Last spring, he wasn't sure if Elway would return for his 16th season, but he trained as if Elway was history.

"No one could put more pressure on me than I put on myself. I don't allow anybody to put pressure on me that I think is unnecessary. I mean, if you start thinking about the pressure on you, that's when you start to crack," he said.

"I still have a lot of work to do. I still have a lot more games to win – hopefully, a lot more Super Bowls to win. If you do those things, I think your name will automatically be pushed as one of the greatest backs of all time.

“"When it's all said and done

and I hang up my cleats for the last time, I'd like to think that I'm the greatest back to play the game.

"But nothing is guaranteed you. I try to play as hard as I can because I don't want to leave anything out there.

I'm on borrowed time."

That's a scary thought to Davis' teammates, who regard him as both a MVP and a close friend. After Davis' run for 2,000 yards, defensive end Neil Smith moved in to scoop up the historic ball.

"Terrell ran to our sideline and he got tackled and I just looked down and there was the ball," he said. "Some young guy grabbed it first and I just took it from him so I could hand it to Terrell."

Added Davis: "If I had left the game with 1,980 yards, I would have been upset. Now the linemen can sit there and talk about blocking for a back that

"When it comes to championships, the coaches know, the players know, and my teammates know I'm ready for the call."

Terrell Davis

ran for 2,000 yards. That's a special feat.

"This is a special team. I know how lucky I am." •

AFC Championship

Denver 23, New York Jets 10

In what might have been John Elway's last game at Mile High Stadium, the Broncos overcame a lackluster first half and dispatched Bill Parcels and the New York Jets by a score of 23-10.

After the Jets took a 10-0 lead three minutes into the second half, the Denver offense exploded for 20 third-quarter points while the Broncos defense put the clamps down on Jets quarterback Vinny Testeverde and the rest of the New York offense.

Although New York outgained Denver in yardage (370-331) and first downs (18-14), the Broncos defense forced six turnovers, which ultimately spelled the Jets' demise.

Denver tied the score as a result of one of the Jets turnovers, a fumbled kickoff recovered by the Broncos at the New York 31-yard line. Jason Elam converted that New York miscue into a 48-yard field goal that tied the game at 10.

After another Elam field goal put Denver ahead for the first time in the game, Davis gave the Broncos some breathing room with a 31-yard touchdown run at the end of the third quarter that put his team ahead 20-10. Denver would add one more field goal in the fourth quarter, and the Jets never seriously threatened in the game's final stanza.

The win propelled the defending NFL champion Broncos into their second consecutive Super Bowl, giving them a chance to become the first AFC team to repeat as NFL champions since the 1978-79 Pittsburgh Steelers. •

#1 Jason Elam

AFC CHAMPIONSHIP GAME

January 17, 1999

Denver 23, NY Jets 10

#51 John Mobley

Box Score

	1st	2nd	3rd	4th	TOTAL
NY Jets	0	3	7	0	10
Denver	*0*	*0*	*20*	*3*	*23*

SCORING

2ND QUARTER

NYJ-FG JOHN HALL 32 YD.

3RD QUARTER

NYJ-TD CURTIS MARTIN 1 YD RUN (JOHN HALL KICK).

DEN-TD HOWARD GRIFFITH 11 YD PASS FROM JOHN ELWAY (JASON ELAM KICK).

DEN-FG JASON ELAM 44 YD.

DEN-FG JASON ELAM 48 YD.

DEN-TD TERRELL DAVIS 31 YD RUN (JASON ELAM KICK).

4TH QUARTER

DEN-FG JASON ELAM 35 YD.

BRONCOS

AFC Playoffs

Denver 38, Miami 3

After missing each other over the previous 13 seasons, legendary quarterbacks John Elway and Dan Marino had already met earlier this year in a game that the Dolphins won, 31-21. The playoffs brought these two star passers together again for the second time this season, but the outcome was entirely different this time around.

The Broncos defense forced Marino into two interceptions and limited the Miami rushing game to just 14 yards while Denver running back Terrell Davis ran for 199 yards and two touchdowns as his Broncos blasted Miami out of the playoffs with a 38-3 win at Mile High Stadium.

Davis' 199-yard performance was the fourth-highest rushing total in NFL playoff history. The performance came just three weeks after the Dolphins held Davis to a season-low 29 yards on 16 carries.

Denver jumped on the Dolphins from the start, taking the opening kickoff and marching 92 yards on 14 plays over 7:56, taking a 7-0 lead on a one-yard run by Davis. The Broncos extended their lead to 14-0 on another scoring run by Davis, this time a 20-yard run just over a minute before the end of the quarter. The Broncos led 21-3 at halftime and were never threatened in the second half. •

AFC PLAYOFF GAME

January 9, 1999

Denver 38, Miami 3

#90
Neil Smith

Box Score

	1st	2nd	3rd	4th	TOTAL
Miami	0	3	0	0	3
Denver	*14*	*7*	*3*	*14*	*38*

SCORING

1ST QUARTER

DEN-TD TERRELL DAVIS 1 YD RUN (JASON ELAM KICK).
DEN-TD TERRELL DAVIS 20 YD RUN (JASON ELAM KICK).

2ND QUARTER

MIA-FG OLINDO MARE 22 YD.
DEN-TD DEREK LOVILLE 11 YD RUN (JASON ELAM KICK).

3RD QUARTER

DEN-FG JASON ELAM 32 YD.

4TH QUARTER

DEN-TD ROD SMITH 28 YD PASS FROM JOHN ELWAY (JASON ELAM KICK).
DEN-TD NEIL SMITH 79 YD FUMBLE RETURN (JASON ELAM KICK).

Game Sixteen

Denver 28, Seattle 21

Denver broke back into the win column with a 28-21 win over Seattle at the King Dome in the season finale for both teams.

Terrell Davis finished the game with 178 yards on 29 carries. His total pushed him over the 2,000-yard mark for the season, making him just the fourth running back in NFL history to do so. More importantly for the Broncos, the win sent them into the playoffs on a winning note.

With Denver already leading 21-7 in the third quarter, the Broncos engineered a 16-play, 88-yard scoring drive that lasted 7:52. The drive ended when John Elway threw a short one-yard scoring toss to Shannon Sharpe that put the Broncos ahead 28-7 with 11:45 left in the game.

But Seattle did not quit. The Seahawks marched 72-yards in five plays on their next possession, cutting the lead to 28-14 on a 7-yard Jon Kitna-to-Mike Pritchard scoring pass with just under six minutes remaining. Seattle sliced the lead even further, pulling to within 28-21 on a late touchdown with just 1:32 remaining, but Denver recovered the ensuing on-side kick and was able to run out the clock.

After being held to just 29 yards a week earlier, Davis came into the game needing 170 yards to break the 2,000-yard mark. He broke the 2,000-yard plateau on a 15-yard run with 8:52 remaining in the game. •

GAME SIXTEEN

December 27, 1998

Denver 28, Seattle 21

2,008 Total Rushing Yds.

#30 Terrell Davis

Box Score

	1st	2nd	3rd	4th	TOTAL
Seattle	7	0	0	14	21
Denver	*0*	*14*	*7*	*7*	*28*

SCORING

1ST QUARTER

SEA-TD RICKY WATTERS 4 YD RUN (TODD PETERSON KICK).

2ND QUARTER

DEN-TD ROD SMITH 33 YD PASS FROM JOHN ELWAY (JASON ELAM KICK).

DEN-TD SHANNON SHARPE 17 YD PASS FROM JOHN ELWAY (JASON ELAM KICK).

3RD QUARTER

DEN-TD TERRELL DAVIS 2 YD PASS FROM JOHN ELWAY (JASON ELAM KICK).

4TH QUARTER

DEN-TD SHANNON SHARPE 1 YD PASS FROM JOHN ELWAY (JASON ELAM KICK).

SEA-TD MIKE PRITCHARD 7 YD PASS FROM JON KITNA (TODD PETERSON KICK).

SEA-TD DEEMS MAY 1 YD PASS FROM RICKY WATTERS (TODD PETER SON KICK).

Game Fifteen

Miami 31, Denver 21

Coming off their first loss of the season, the Broncos traveled to Miami for a game that featured the first matchup between quarterbacks John Elway and Dan Marino in 13 years. At the end of the much-hyped matchup, it was Marino who won the quarterback duel, throwing for 355 yards and four touchdowns as Miami won 31-21.

Denver led 13-7 at halftime, but the second half was all Miami. The Dolphins took their first lead at 14-13 when Marino connected with Lamar Thomas in the end zone and a 56-yard toss just four-and-a-half minutes into the third quarter. The lead ballooned to 21-13 five minutes later after Marino again found Thomas in the end zone, this time on a 17-yard pass.

Miami appeared to ice the game when Marino threw his fourth touchdown pass of the game, giving the Dolphins a 28-13 advantage with 7:15 remaining. But Denver got right back into the game on the ensuing kickoff after Vaughn Hebron returned the kick 95 yards for a touchdown. Denver's two-point conversion was successful, and the lead was cut to 28-21. But the Broncos could get no closer, and Miami's Olindo Mare added a 42-yard field goal with 1:50 remaining to clinch the victory.

Miami's defense held Terrell Davis to just 29 yards on 16 carries, while Dolphin wide receiver Lamar Thomas racked up three touchdowns and 136 yards on six catches. •

GAME FIFTEEN

December 21, 1998

Miami 31, Denver 21

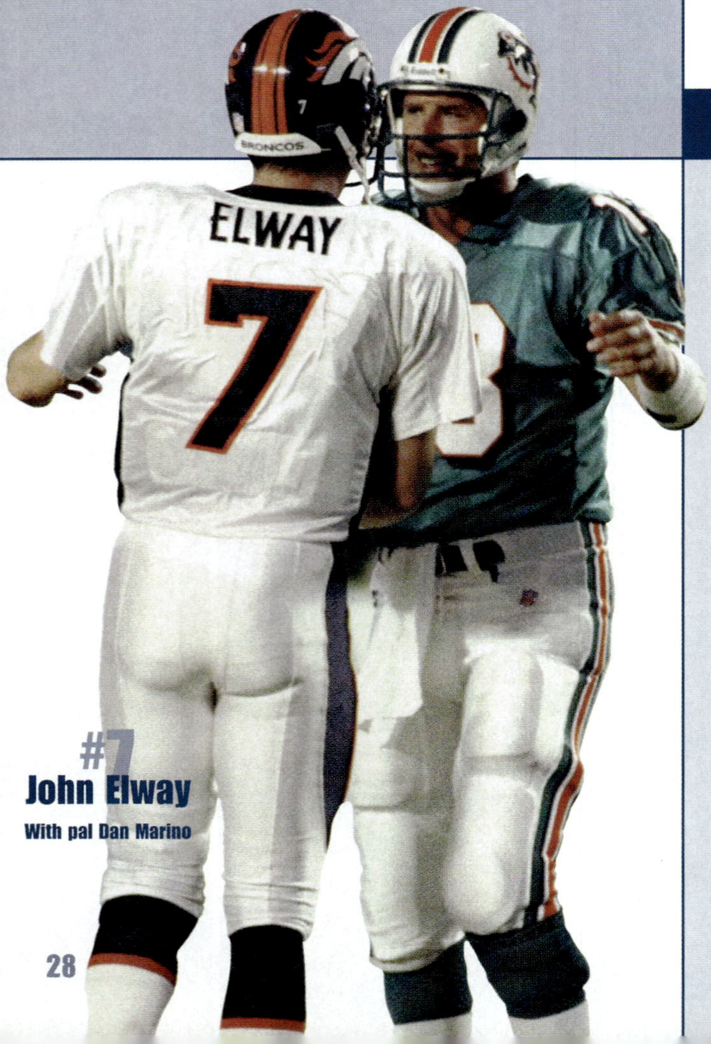

#7
John Elway
With pal Dan Marino

Box Score

	1st	2nd	3rd	4th	TOTAL
Denver	*3*	*10*	*0*	*8*	*21*
Miami	0	7	14	10	31

SCORING

1ST QUARTER
DEN-FG JASON ELAM 52 YD.

2ND QUARTER
DEN-TD ROD SMITH RECOVERED FUMBLE IN END ZONE (JASON ELAM KICK).
MIA-TD LAMAR THOMAS 9 YD PASS FROM DAN MARINO (OLINDO MARE KICK).
DEN-FG JASON ELAM 44 YD.

3RD QUARTER
MIA-TD LAMAR THOMAS 56 YD PASS FROM DAN MARINO (OLINDO MARE KICK).
MIA-TD LAMAR THOMAS 17 YD PASS FROM DAN MARINO (OLINDO MARE KICK).

4TH QUARTER
MIA-TD ORONDE GADSDEN 8 YD PASS FROM DAN MARINO (OLINDO MARE KICK).
DEN-TD VAUGHN HEBRON 95 YD KICKOFF RETURN (BUBBY BRISTER PASS TO ED MCCAFFREY FOR TWO-POINT CONVERSION).
MIA-FG OLINDO MARE 42 YD.

MADISON

MADISO

Game Fourteen

N.Y. Giants 20, Denver 16

A struggling New York Giants football team drove 86 yards on a miraculous scoring drive and ended the Denver Broncos' dream of becoming the NFL's first undefeated team since the 1972 Miami Dolphins.

With Denver clinging to a 16-13 lead, the Giants took the ball at their own 14-yard line with just 2:39 remaining in the game. The odds seemed stacked against New York, but the Giants responded with a remarkable six-play, 86-yard drive that allowed them to pull out the win. New York quarterback Kent Graham found Joe Jurevicius for an 11-yard completion on third-and-10 on a crucial play that allowed the Giants' drive to continue. Graham then found Giants' receiver Amani Toomer in the end zone for a 37-yard TD pass that put New York ahead 20-16 with just 48 seconds left. A packed Giants Stadium went wild as their team recorded one of its biggest victories of the decade.

The win dropped Denver to 13-1 on the season and snapped the team's winning streak at 18 games – just one short of the league record. The loss also dashed the Broncos' hopes of joining the 1972 Miami Dolphins (17-0) as the only team in NFL history to complete an undefeated and untied season. Ironically, the NFL schedule would have allowed Denver to continue that quest against the Dolphins as the Broncos next game would be on the road at Miami.

Terrell Davis rushed 28 times for 147 yards for Denver in the losing cause, while John Elway was 19-of-36 for 180 yards and an interception. •

GAME FOURTEEN

December 13, 1998

NY Giants 20, Denver 16

#22
Vaughn Hebron

Box Score

	1st	2nd	3rd	4th	TOTAL
Denver	*3*	*3*	*3*	*7*	*16*
NY Giants	3	7	0	10	20

SCORING

1ST QUARTER

DEN-FG JASON ELAM 24 YD.

NYG-FG BRAD DALUISO 36 YD.

2ND QUARTER

DEN-FG JASON ELAM 38 YD.

NYG-TD TIKI BARBER 21 YD PASS FROM KENT GRAHAM (BRAD DALUISO KICK).

3RD QUARTER

DEN-FG JASON ELAM 30 YD.

4TH QUARTER

NYG-FG BRAD DALUISO 19 YD.

DEN-TD TERRELL DAVIS 27 YD RUN (JASON ELAM KICK).

NYG-TD AMANI TOOMER 37 YD PASS FROM KENT GRAHAM (BRAD DALUISO KICK).

HESS
First Union
Budweiser

Game Thirteen

Denver 35, Kansas City 31

Denver rallied for two touchdowns in the final seven minutes to beat Kansas City 35-31 while keeping their hopes alive for a perfect season.

The Chiefs roared out of the opening gate, leaving Denver in unfamiliar territory as Kansas City rolled to a 21-7 first-quarter advantage. The Broncos came back to knot the score at 21 going into halftime, but the Chiefs seemed determined to leave Mile High Stadium with the victory.

Kansas City quarterback Rich Gannon hit Joe Horn on a 26-yard touchdown pass to give the Chiefs a 28-21 lead with 3:40 left in the third quarter. Kansas City's lead grew to 10 on a 20-yard Pete Stoyanovich field goal that put the Chiefs up 31-21. With just 8:25 remaining in the game, it appeared that the Broncos' perfect season was about to come to an end.

But John Elway and the Broncos wouldn't go down without a fight. On Denver's next possession, Elway hit Willie Green on a 50-yard bomb that gave Denver 1st-and-goal at the Kansas City one. Terrell Davis rumbled into the end zone for his third touchdown of the game, slicing the Chiefs' lead to 31-28 with 6:48 left in the game.

Denver clinched the victory on its next possession, mounting a five-play, 50-yard drive that culminated with a 24-yard Elway-to-Shannon Sharpe scoring toss that put the Broncos ahead for good with 3:34 remaining.

Elway finished the game with 400 yards on 22-of-32 passing, his first 400-yard effort since December 20, 1985.

The win allowed Denver to become just the third team in NFL history to begin a season with 13 consecutive wins. It also extended the Broncos' win streak to 18 games, tying a league record. •

GAME THIRTEEN

December 6, 1998

Denver 35, Kansas City 31

#84
Shannon Sharpe

Box Score

	1st	2nd	3rd	4th	TOTAL
Kansas City	21	0	7	3	31
Denver	7	14	0	14	35

SCORING

1ST QUARTER

KAN-TD ANDRE RISON 26 YD PASS FROM RICH GANNON (PETE STOYANOVICH KICK).
KAN-TD KIMBLE ANDERS 11 YD PASS FROM RICH GANNON (PETE STOYANOVICH KICK).
DEN-TD TERRELL DAVIS 1 YD RUN (JASON ELAM KICK).
KAN-TD BAM MORRIS 1 YD RUN (PETE STOYANOVICH KICK).

2ND QUARTER

DEN-TD TERRELL DAVIS 1 YD RUN (JASON ELAM KICK).
DEN-TD ED MCCAFFREY 13 YD PASS FROM JOHN ELWAY (JASON ELAM KICK).

3RD QUARTER

KAN-TD JOE HORN 26 YD PASS FROM RICH GANNON (PETE STOYANOVICH KICK).

4TH QUARTER

KAN-FG PETE STOYANOVICH 20 YD.
DEN-TD TERRELL DAVIS 1 YD RUN (JASON ELAM KICK).
DEN-TD SHANNON SHARPE 24 YD PASS FROM JOHN ELWAY (JASON ELAM KICK).

Game Twelve

Denver 31, San Diego 16

Denver returned to San Diego's Qualcomm Stadium and the site of its Super Bowl XXXII victory over Green Bay. Like the stadium, the results were familiar for the Broncos – another victory.

The Broncos moved to 11-0 as John Elway threw four touchdown passes in Denver's 31-16 rout of the Chargers. Thanks to the Raiders' loss to Washington earlier in the day, the Broncos took the field having already clinched the AFC West championship.

Terrell Davis was held in check for the second time in four weeks, rushing for 74 yards on 24 carries. The Chargers defense kept Davis out of the end zone.

While San Diego kept Denver from rushing into the end zone, the Chargers couldn't keep the Broncos from throwing into it. Elway connected on touchdown passes of 15, 17, 13 and 18 yards for Denver. While he completed 19-of-34 passes for 239 yards, Elway's four scoring strikes helped overcome three interceptions.

Denver receiver Rod Smith had a big game for the Broncos, snagging eight catches for 101 yards. He scored on a 13-yard touchdown pass from Elway that put Denver ahead 21-10 in the second quarter. •

GAME TWELVE

November 29, 1998

Denver 31, San Diego 16

#98
Maa Tanuvasa

Box Score

	1st	2nd	3rd	4th	TOTAL
Denver	*14*	*7*	*7*	*3*	*31*
San Diego	10	0	0	6	16

SCORING

1ST QUARTER

SD-FG JOHN CARNEY 27 YD.
DEN-TD ED MCCAFFREY 15 YD PASS FROM JOHN ELWAY (JASON ELAM KICK).
DEN-TD ED MCCAFFREY 37 YD PASS FROM JOHN ELWAY (JASON ELAM KICK).
SD-TD TERRELL FLETCHER 13 YD RUN (JOHN CARNEY KICK).

2ND QUARTER

DEN-TD ROD SMITH 13 YD PASS FROM JOHN ELWAY (JASON ELAM KICK).

3RD QUARTER

DEN-TD SHANNON SHARPE 18 YD PASS FROM JOHN ELWAY (JASON ELAM KICK).

4TH QUARTER

DEN-FG JASON ELAM 34 YD.
SD-TD BRYAN STILL 47 YD PASS FROM CRAIG WHELIHAN (TWO-POINT CONVERSION FAILED).

WHELIHAN
McKENZIE

BRONCOS

Game Eleven

Denver 40, Oakland 14

John Elway returned to the starting lineup and helped the Broncos clinch a playoff berth by laying a 40-14 shellacking on the Oakland Raiders at Mile High Stadium. In the process, Elway became just the second quarterback in NFL history to throw for more than 50,000 yards in his career.

With the win, Denver became just the 10th NFL team ever to start a season 11-0, leading some players to openly speculate for the first time on the Broncos' chances of matching the 1972 Dolphins' unbeaten run through the regular season.

But the 11th win wasn't in the bag for Denver until the fourth quarter. After the Broncos jumped out to a 17-0 lead, Oakland clawed back to 17-14 by the end of the third quarter. Then Denver put the game away, exploding for 23 fourth-quarter points to come away with the 26-point victory.

Jason Elam kicked off the fourth-quarter scoring with a 23-yard field goal to put Denver up by six, 20-14. Oakland quarterback Donald Hollas threw an interception at his own 36 on the Raiders' next possession, setting up a 28-yard touchdown pass from Elway to Rod Smith just two minutes later that increased the Broncos' margin to 27-14. •

GAME ELEVEN

November 22, 1998

Denver 40, Oakland 14

#89
Dwayne Carswell

Box Score

	1st	2nd	3rd	4th	TOTAL
Oakland	0	7	7	0	14
Denver	*3*	*14*	*0*	*23*	*40*

SCORING

1ST QUARTER
DEN-FG JASON ELAM 33 YD.

2ND QUARTER
DEN-TD SHANNON SHARPE 7 YD PASS FROM JOHN ELWAY (JASON ELAM KICK).
DEN-TD TERRELL DAVIS 1 YD RUN (JASON ELAM KICK).
OAK-TD RICKEY DUDLEY 29 YD PASS FROM DONALD HOLLAS (GREG DAVIS KICK).

3RD QUARTER
OAK-TD JAMES JETT 14 YD PASS FROM DONALD HOLLAS (GREG DAVIS KICK).

4TH QUARTER
DEN-FG JASON ELAM 23 YD.
DEN-TD ROD SMITH 28 YD PASS FROM JOHN ELWAY (TWO-POINT CONVERSION FAILED).
DEN-TD HOWARD GRIFFITH 3 YD PASS FROM JOHN ELWAY (JASON ELAM KICK).
DEN-TD VAUGHN HEBRON 3 YD RUN (JASON ELAM KICK).

Riddell
83
BRONCOS

83
86
22
53
29

Game Ten

Denver 30, Kansas City 7

Denver routed AFC West rival Kansas City 30-7 to become the first team since the 1991 Washington Redskins to start a season 10-0.

Backup quarterback Bubby Brister again got the nod, making his second consecutive start for an injured John Elway. Brister didn't waste any time making his presence felt, scampering 38 yards for a touchdown just 2:42 into the game to give the Broncos a 7-0 lead.

In sticking to the script that it had followed most of the season, Denver scored again just five minutes later to once again bolt to a large lead early in the game. Against Kansas City, it was a 41-yard run by Terrell Davis that put Denver up 14-0 just 7:24 into the game.

The Chiefs cut the lead to 14-7 when Kansas City quarterback Rich Gannon found Kimble Anders for a three-yard scoring pass, but two Jason Elam field goals increased Denver's lead to 20-7 by halftime.

The Denver defense clamped down in the second half, and the Chiefs could get no closer. Kansas City managed just 31 rushing yards while the Broncos sacked Gannon four times.

Davis got back over the 100-yard mark after being held to a season-low 69 yards the week before. He finished the game with 111 yards on 18 carries. •

GAME TEN

November 16, 1998

Denver 30, Kansas City 7

#6
Bubby Brister

Box Score

	1st	2nd	3rd	4th	TOTAL
Denver	*14*	*6*	*3*	*7*	*30*
Kansas City	0	7	0	0	7

SCORING

1ST QUARTER
DEN-TD BUBBY BRISTER 38 YD RUN (JASON ELAM KICK).
DEN-TD TERRELL DAVIS 41 YD RUN (JASON ELAM KICK).

2ND QUARTER
KAN-TD KIMBLE ANDERS 3 YD PASS FROM RICH GANNON (PETE STOYANOVICH KICK).
DEN-FG JASON ELAM 42 YD.
DEN-FG JASON ELAM 46 YD.

3RD QUARTER
DEN-FG JASON ELAM 35 YD.

4TH QUARTER
DEN-TD DEREK LOVILLE 2 YD RUN (JASON ELAM KICK)

Game Nine

Denver 27, San Diego 10

Denver put away another opponent early in the game, this time jumping out to a 20-0 halftime lead to beat San Diego 27-10.

Terrell Davis opened the scoring for Denver, snagging a four-yard toss from backup quarterback Bubby Brister to put the Broncos ahead 7-0 in the first quarter. Davis reached the end zone again, this time scoring on a 24-yard run with 2:39 left in the first half, putting Denver up 17-0. A 26-yard field goal by Jason Elam with four seconds left in the half gave Denver a 20-0 halftime advantage.

Denver upped its lead to 27-0 on a Brister-to-Ed McCaffrey scoring strike early in the third. The score was set up by a Darrien Gordon interception, which he returned 36 yards to the San Diego 7.

Brister made a surprise start for the Broncos after John Elway suffered a minor injury during the pregame warmups. As he had previously in the season, Brister filled in nicely for Elway, completing 20-of-33 passes for 229 yards, two touchdowns and one interception.

While Brister put up impressive numbers at quarterback, running back Terrell Davis was held to a season-low 69 yards on 20 carries. However, he still scored touchdowns for the Broncos. •

GAME NINE

November 8, 1998

Denver 27, San Diego 10

Box Score

	1st	2nd	3rd	4th	TOTAL
San Diego	0	0	0	10	10
Denver	*7*	*13*	*7*	*0*	*27*

SCORING

1ST QUARTER

DEN-TD TERRELL DAVIS 4 YD PASS FROM BUBBY BRISTER (JASON ELAM KICK).

2ND QUARTER

DEN-FG JASON ELAM 31 YD.

DEN-TD TERRELL DAVIS 24 YD RUN (JASON ELAM KICK).

DEN-FG JASON ELAM 26 YD.

3RD QUARTER

DEN-TD ED MCCAFFREY 7 YD PASS FROM BUBBY BRISTER (JASON ELAM KICK).

4TH QUARTER

SD-TD FREDDIE JONES 14 YD PASS FROM CRAIG WHELIHAN (CRAIG WHELIHAN RUN FOR TWO-POINT CONVERSION).

Coach
Mike Shanahan

BRONCOS
86

Riddell
84

BRONCOS
96
55

Game Eight

Denver 33, Cincinnati 26

After opening the season with seven straight victories, the Broncos received a scare the day after Halloween at Cincinnati's Riverfront Stadium.

A sloppy first half sent Denver into the locker room trailing 12-6 at the half. But the Broncos came out in the second half and quickly took the lead. John Elway threw for 50 yards during a seven-play, 74-yard scoring drive that put the Broncos in front for the first time at 13-12.

The Bengals, however, weren't ready to concede defeat. Cincinnati quarterback Neil O'Donnell found James Hundon in the end zone on an 11-yard pass three minutes into the fourth quarter, putting the Bengals back in front 18-13.

Denver rallied again, reclaiming the lead 19-18 on a two-yard run by Terrell Davis with seven minutes to go in the game. Denver extended the lead to 26-18 on its next possession when Elway hit Ed McCaffrey on a 25-yard touchdown strike.

Still, the Bengals were not done. Cincinnati drove 64 yards in 2:10, scoring a touchdown and completing the subsequent two-point conversion to tie the game at 26 with 2:54 remaining.

But the Broncos' Davis showed why is one of the top players in the league, finding the end zone on a five-yard touchdown run, putting Denver ahead for good at 33-26 with 58 seconds remaining in the game. Davis finished with 149 yards on 27 carries. •

GAME EIGHT

November 1, 1998

Denver 33, Cincinnati 26

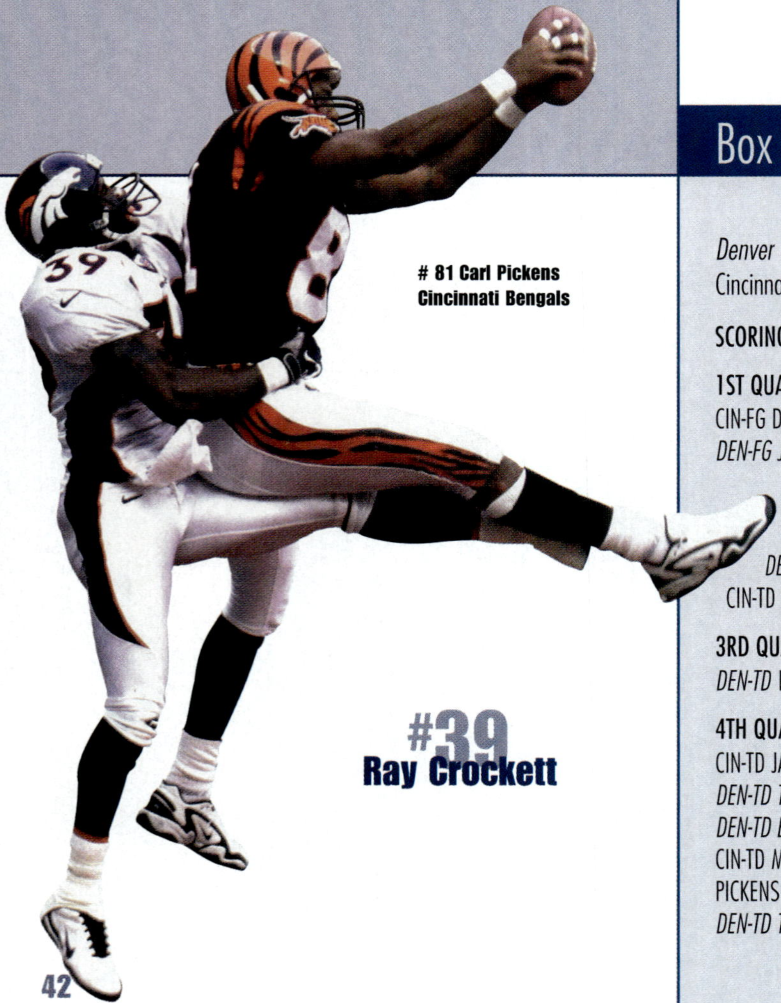

 # 81 Carl Pickens
Cincinnati Bengals

#39
Ray Crockett

Box Score

	1st	2nd	3rd	4th	TOTAL
Denver	*3*	*3*	*7*	*20*	*33*
Cincinnati	3	9	0	14	26

SCORING

1ST QUARTER

CIN-FG DOUG PELFREY 25 YD.

DEN-FG JASON ELAM 33 YD.

2ND QUARTER

CIN-FG DOUG PELFREY 23 YD.

DEN-FG JASON ELAM 37 YD.

CIN-TD DAMON GIBSON 17 YD PASS FROM NEIL ODONNELL (PAT FAILED).

3RD QUARTER

DEN-TD WILLIE GREEN 17 YD PASS FROM JOHN ELWAY (JASON ELAM KICK).

4TH QUARTER

CIN-TD JAMES HUNDON 11 YD PASS FROM NEIL ODONNELL (TWO-POINT CONVERSION FAILED).

DEN-TD TERRELL DAVIS 2 YD RUN (TWO-POINT CONVERSION FAILED).

DEN-TD ED MCCAFFREY 25 YD PASS FROM JOHN ELWAY (JASON ELAM KICK).

CIN-TD MARCO BATTAGLIA 1 YD PASS FROM NEIL ODONNELL (NEIL ODONNELL PASS TO CARL PICKENS FOR TWO-POINT CONVERSION).

DEN-TD TERRELL DAVIS 5 YD RUN (JASON ELAM KICK).

Game Seven

Denver 37, Jacksonville 24

A much-hyped battle between AFC division leaders Denver and Jacksonville turned out to be a flop. Denver jumped on Jacksonville early, taking a 27-10 halftime lead en route to a convincing 37-24 win against the Jaguars.

The Denver offense again racked up some impressive numbers against a highly-regarded Jacksonville defense. Terrell Davis rushed for 136 yards to become just the third running back in NFL history to rush for 1,000 yards in his first seven games. He also caught five passes for 76 yards. John Elway threw to the tune of 295 yards and a touchdown on 21-of-35 passing.

Even kicker Jason Elam got into the act, tying an NFL record by booting a 63-yard field goal on the final play of the first half.

Jacksonville managed to cut the Denver advantage to 27-17 nine minutes into the third quarter, but Davis scored his third touchdown of the day after breaking a tackle and racing 37 yards into the end zone, to push the Bronco lead back to a more comfortable 17 points.

Davis joined Hall of Famers O.J. Simpson and Jim Brown as the only players to ever record 1,000 yards in the first seven games of a season. •

GAME SEVEN

October 25, 1998

Denver 37, Jacksonville 24

Box Score

	1st	2nd	3rd	4th	TOTAL
Jacksonville	3	7	7	7	24
Denver	*3*	*24*	*0*	*10*	*37*

SCORING

1ST QUARTER

DEN-FG JASON ELAM 31 YD.

JAC-FG MIKE HOLLIS 45 YD.

2ND QUARTER

DEN-TD ED MCCAFFREY 41 YD PASS FROM JOHN ELWAY (JASON ELAM KICK).

DEN-TD TERRELL DAVIS 4 YD RUN (JASON ELAM KICK).

JAC-TD FRED TAYLOR 4 YD PASS FROM MARK BRUNELL (MIKE HOLLIS KICK).

DEN-TD TERRELL DAVIS 1 YD RUN (JASON ELAM KICK).

DEN-FG JASON ELAM 63 YD.

3RD QUARTER

JAC-TD DAMON JONES 31 YD PASS FROM MARK BRUNELL (MIKE HOLLIS KICK).

4TH QUARTER

DEN-TD TERRELL DAVIS 37 YD RUN (JASON ELAM KICK).

JAC-TD PETE MITCHELL 2 YD PASS FROM MARK BRUNELL (MIKE HOLLIS KICK).

DEN-FG JASON ELAM 32 YD.

JOYNER

Game Six

Denver 21, Seattle 16

Denver won its sixth game in a row as Terrell Davis rushed for 208 yards and a touchdown in the Broncos' 21-16 win against Seattle at the Kingdome.

Denver again was strong in the first quarter, racing to an early 14-0 lead against Seattle on 50- and 19-yard John Elway touchdown passes to Rod Smith and Shannon Sharpe, respectively. But the lead would not hold up like it did against the hapless Eagles a week earlier.

Seattle's Darrin Smith scored on a 23-yard interception return with just 52 second remaining in the first half, cutting the Broncos' lead to 14-7 while breathing new life into the Seahawks. Todd Peterson then nailed a 23-yard field goal six minutes into the second half, slicing Denver's lead to 14-10.

Davis gave Denver some breathing room a little over one minute into the fourth quarter, diving into the end zone from two yards out to put the Broncos up 21-10.

The Seahawks had one last gasp. Starting at their own 23-yard line with 7:48 remaining, Seattle completed a six-play, 77-yard scoring drive when quarterback John Friesz hit Mike Pritchard on a 50-yard touchdown pass, drawing the Seahawks to within 21-16.

But Davis put the game out of reach for the Broncos. Davis rushed twice for seven yards before breaking to the outside around the left corner, running for 70 yards to the Seattle five and allowing Denver to run out the clock. •

GAME SIX

October 11, 1998

Denver 21, Seattle 16

#29
Howard Griffith

Box Score

	1st	2nd	3rd	4th	TOTAL
Denver	14	0	0	7	21
Seattle	0	7	3	6	16

SCORING

1ST QUARTER

DEN-TD ROD SMITH 50 YD PASS FROM JOHN ELWAY (JASON ELAM KICK).
DEN-TD SHANNON SHARPE 19 YD PASS FROM JOHN ELWAY (JASON ELAM KICK).

2ND QUARTER

SEA-TD DARRIN SMITH 23 YD INTERCEPTION RETURN (TODD PETERSON KICK).

3RD QUARTER

SEA-FG TODD PETERSON 23 YD.

4TH QUARTER

DEN-TD TERRELL DAVIS 2 YD RUN (JASON ELAM KICK).
SEA-TD MIKE PRITCHARD 50 YD PASS FROM JOHN FRIESZ (TWO-POINT CONVERSION FAILED).

Game Five

Denver 41, Philadelphia 16

Denver wasted little time in dispatching out-manned Philadelphia. Denver rolled to early leads of 28-0 and 41-2 before completing its 41-16 thrashing of the Eagles.

Bubby Brister started again in relief of John Elway, matching a career-high with four touchdown passes while Terrell Davis rushed for 168 yards and two touchdowns. Denver put on an offensive clinic in the first quarter, with Davis scoring on runs of 20- and one-yard while Brister threw for two touchdowns as the Broncos built a 28-0 advantage.

Things didn't get any better in the second and third quarters for the Eagles, as Denver ended the second quarter with a 35-2 lead and went into the fourth quarter up 41-2. Philadelphia managed to break into double digits only when Charlie Garner found the end zone with a scant three seconds remaining on the clock.

The Denver defense was also in top form, holding the Eagles to 12 first downs and just 157 yards of total offense. By contract, the Broncos tallied 22 first downs and 423 yards of offense. Brister finished with 203 of those yards on 16-of-29 passing. •

GAME FIVE

October 4, 1998

Denver 41, Philadelphia 16

#93
Trevor Pryce

Box Score

	1st	2nd	3rd	4th	TOTAL
Philadelphia	0	2	0	14	16
Denver	*28*	*7*	*6*	*0*	*41*

SCORING

1ST QUARTER

DEN-TD TERRELL DAVIS 20 YD RUN (JASON ELAM KICK).

DEN-TD ROD SMITH 8 YD PASS FROM BUBBY BRISTER (JASON ELAM KICK).

DEN-TD SHANNON SHARPE 9 YD PASS FROM BUBBY BRISTER (JASON ELAM KICK).

DEN-TD TERRELL DAVIS 1 YD RUN (JASON ELAM KICK).

DEN-TD ED MCCAFFREY 12 YD PASS FROM BUBBY BRISTER (JASON ELAM KICK).

3RD QUARTER

DEN-TD ROD SMITH 31 YD PASS FROM BUBBY BRISTER (PAT FAILED).

4TH QUARTER

PHI-TD CHARLIE GARNER 3 YD RUN (CHRIS BONIOL KICK).

PHI-TD CHARLIE GARNER 3 YD RUN (CHRIS BONIOL KICK).

BRONCOS

BRONCOS

Game Four

Denver 38, Washington 16

Another 100-yard rushing game by Terrell Davis and a solid performance by backup quarterback Bubby Brister offset the absence of John Elway as the Broncos walloped the Washington Redskins 38-16 to remain undefeated at 4-0.

Denver scored on its first two possessions, including a seven-play, 81-yard opening drive that was capped by a 19-yard Brister-to-Ed McCaffrey pass that put the Broncos up 7-0. It was just the begging of a solid, mistake-free game for Brister, who completed 16-of-24 passes in the game for 180 yards and two touchdowns.

Terrell Davis didn't hit pay-dirt until the third quarter, but when he finally did get into the end zone, it was in most impressive fashion. Davis rumbled 42 yards for the score less than two minutes into the second half, giving Denver a 24-7 lead. Any hopes for a Redskin comeback were dashed six minutes later when Brister found Howard Griffith in the end zone for his second touchdown pass of the game, putting the Broncos up 31-7.

Davis finished the game with 119 yards and a touchdown on 21 carries. It was his third-straight 100-yard rushing game.

The win was the Broncos' first in nine years when starting a quarterback other than Elway. Denver was 0-7 without starting Elway since beating, ironically, Washington, 14-10 in 1989. •

GAME FOUR

September 27, 1998

Denver 38, Washington 16

Box Score

	1st	2nd	3rd	4th	TOTAL
Denver	*7*	*10*	*14*	*7*	*38*
Washington	0	7	3	6	16

SCORING

1ST QUARTER

DEN-TD ED MCCAFFREY 19 YD PASS FROM BUBBY BRISTER (JASON ELAM KICK).

2ND QUARTER

DEN-FG JASON ELAM 37 YD.

DEN-TD DARRIEN GORDON 55 YD INTERCEPTION RETURN (JASON ELAM KICK).

WAS-TD TERRY ALLEN 5 YD RUN (CARY BLANCHARD KICK).

3RD QUARTER

DEN-TD TERRELL DAVIS 42 YD RUN (JASON ELAM KICK).

DEN-TD HOWARD GRIFFITH 14 YD PASS FROM BUBBY BRISTER (JASON ELAM KICK).

WAS-FG CARY BLANCHARD 37 YD.

4TH QUARTER

DEN-TD DEREK LOVILLE 1 YD RUN (JASON ELAM KICK).

WAS-TD MICHAEL WESTBROOK 75 YD PASS FROM TRENT GREEN (TWO-POINT CONVERSION FAIL

#29 Howard Griffith

#31 Derek Loville

Game Three

Denver 34, Oakland 17

Backup quarterback Bubby Brister relieved an injured John Elway and threw for two touchdowns to lead Denver to a 34-17 victory over the archrival Oakland Raiders.

Brister, who entered the game after Elway aggravated his right hamstring in the second quarter, got off to a shaky start. His first pass attempt was intercepted by Oakland's Eric Turner and returned 94 yards to give the Raiders a 10-7 lead with just under seven minutes remaining in the first half.

But it didn't take long for the veteran Brister to shake off the rust, directing Denver on two scoring drives to send the Broncos into the locker room back on top with a 17-10 advantage. A 15-yard run on 3rd-and-8 kept a nine-play, 43-yard drive going for Denver, which resulted in a 35-yard Jason Elam field goal that knotted the score at 10. On the Broncos' subsequent possession, Brister again kept the Denver offense on the field, scrambling for a two-yard gain on a 3rd-and-1 to get the first down. Brister finished the drive with a three-yard touchdown toss to Howard Griffith to put Denver up, 17-10.

Brister threw his second touchdown pass eight minutes into the third quarter, a 13-yard pass to Ed McCaffrey to stretch the lead to 24-10. He finished the game 10-of-17 for 140 yards, two touchdowns and one interception. •

GAME THREE

September 20, 1998

Denver 34, Oakland 17

Box Score

	1st	2nd	3rd	4th	TOTAL
Denver	*7*	*10*	*7*	*10*	*34*
Oakland	0	10	7	0	17

SCORING

1ST QUARTER

DEN-TD ED MCCAFFREY 1 YD PASS FROM JOHN ELWAY (JASON ELAM KICK).

2ND QUARTER

OAK-FG GREG DAVIS 44 YD.

OAK-TD ERIC TURNER 94 YD INTERCEPTION RETURN (GREG DAVIS KICK).

DEN-FG JASON ELAM 35 YD.

DEN-TD HOWARD GRIFFITH 3 YD PASS FROM BUBBY BRISTER (JASON ELAM KICK).

3RD QUARTER

DEN-TD ED MCCAFFREY 13 YD PASS FROM BUBBY BRISTER (JASON ELAM KICK).

OAK-TD RICKEY DUDLEY 11 YD PASS FROM JEFF GEORGE (GREG DAVIS KICK).

4TH QUARTER

DEN-FG JASON ELAM 35 YD.

DEN-TD RAY CROCKETT 80 YD INTERCEPTION RETURN (JASON ELAM KICK).

BRONCOS

Game Two

Denver 42, Dallas 23

After finally breaking the AFC's long Super Bowl title drought, many questioned whether the Broncos would again be a legitimate contender again in 1998. With the Dallas Cowboys visiting Mile High Stadium in the second week of the season, Denver had a chance to show what it was made of. And did they ever.

Denver scored touchdowns on all five of its first half possessions, shredding the Cowboy defense for 35 points as Denver piled up a 35-17 halftime advantage. Davis ran at will against the Dallas defense, scoring on runs of 63 and 59 yards en route to amassing 177 yards in the first half alone. John Elway was also hot in the first half, connecting on 11-of-13 passes for 217 yards and two touchdowns.

Denver set the tone early, with Elway completing four-of-four passes as the Broncos marched 84 yards in seven plays on their opening drive. Elway capped the drive with a 38-yard pass to Shannon Sharpe for the early 7-0 lead. Denver then closed the first quarter with Davis scoring twice on his 63- and 59-yard runs as the Broncos upped their lead to 21-7. The rest of the game was all Denver, which finished with 515 yards of total offense, the fifth-highest mark in franchise history. •

GAME TWO

September 13, 1998

Denver 42, Dallas 23

#80

Rod Smith

Box Score

	1st	2nd	3rd	4th	TOTAL
Dallas	7	10	3	3	23
Denver	*21*	*14*	*0*	*7*	*42*

SCORING

1ST QUARTER

DEN-TD SHANNON SHARPE 38 YD PASS FROM JOHN ELWAY (JASON ELAM KICK).
DAL-TD ERNIE MILLS 36 YD PASS FROM TROY AIKMAN (RICHIE CUNNINGHAM KICK).
DEN-TD TERRELL DAVIS 63 YD RUN (JASON ELAM KICK).
DEN-TD TERRELL DAVIS 59 YD RUN (JASON ELAM KICK).

2ND QUARTER

DAL-TD EMMITT SMITH 4 YD RUN (RICHIE CUNNINGHAM KICK).
DEN-TD SHANNON SHARPE 23 YD PASS FROM JOHN ELWAY (JASON ELAM KICK).
DAL-FG RICHIE CUNNINGHAM 30 YD.
DEN-TD JOHN ELWAY 1 YD RUN (JASON ELAM KICK).

3RD QUARTER

DAL-FG RICHIE CUNNINGHAM 54 YD.

4TH QUARTER

DAL-FG RICHIE CUNNINGHAM 26 YD.
DEN-TD TERRELL DAVIS 3 YD RUN (JASON ELAM KICK).

Game One

Denver 27, New England 21

Terrell Davis and John Elway picked up right where they left off in Super Bowl XXXII, combining for three touchdowns to lead the defending-champion Broncos to a 27-21 season-opening Monday night win against the New England Patriots.

Elway hit receiver Shannon Sharpe on a 12-yard scoring strike at the end of the first quarter and Davis added a nine-yard touchdown run seven minutes later as Denver bolted to an early 17-0 advantage. The Patriots pulled to within 17-14 on a 24-yard Drew Bledsoe-to-Troy Brown touchdown pass just over two minutes into the second half, but the Broncos would not let New England get any closer.

After a third quarter 42-yard field goal by kicker Jason Elam gave Denver a 20-14 lead, Davis put the game away for the Broncos. He capped an eight-play, 43-yard drive with a one-yard touchdown plunge that put his team ahead 27-14.

The Patriots would not get on the board again until Bledsoe found Vincent Brisby in the end zone with less than two minutes remaining in the game. Out of timeouts, New England could not recover the onside kick, allowing the 27-21 margin to stand for the Broncos.

Elway finished the game 22-of-34 for 257 yards and one touchdown. Davis rushed 22 times for 75 yards, scoring twice for Denver. •

GAME ONE

September 7, 1998

Denver 27, New England 21

#7 John Elway

Box Score

	1st	2nd	3rd	4th	TOTAL
New England	0	7	7	7	21
Denver	*10*	*7*	*3*	*7*	*27*

SCORING

1ST QUARTER

DEN-FG JASON ELAM 53 YD.

DEN-TD SHANNON SHARPE 12 YD PASS FROM JOHN ELWAY (JASON ELAM KICK).

2ND QUARTER

DEN-TD TERRELL DAVIS 9 YD RUN (JASON ELAM KICK).

NE-TD ROBERT EDWARDS 1 YD RUN (ADAM VINATIERI KICK).

3RD QUARTER

NE-TD TROY BROWN 24 YD PASS FROM DREW BLEDSOE (ADAM VINATIERI KICK).

DEN-FG JASON ELAM 42 YD.

4TH QUARTER

DEN-TD TERRELL DAVIS 1 YD RUN (JASON ELAM KICK).

NE-TD VINCENT BRISBY 10 YD PASS FROM DREW BLEDSOE (ADAM VINATIERI KICK)

BRONCOS
93
21

BLEDSOE
11

32

1998-99 Denver Broncos Statistics

SCORING

	Tot. TD	Rush	Rec.	FG	PAT	S	Pts.
Terrell Davis	23	21	2	0/0	0/0	0	138
Jason Elam	0	0	0	23/27	58/58	0	127
Ed McCaffrey	10	0	10	0/0	0/0	0	62
Shannon Sharpe	10	0	10	0/0	0/0	0	60
Rod Smith	7	0	6	0/0	0/0	0	42
Howard Griffith	3	0	3	0/0	0/0	0	18
Vaughn Hebron	2	1	0	0/0	0/0	0	12
Derek Loville	2	2	0	0/0	0/0	0	12
Bubby Brister	1	1	0	0/0	0/0	0	6
Ray Crockett	1	0	0	0/0	0/0	0	6
John Elway	1	1	0	0/0	0/0	0	6
Darrien Gordon	1	0	0	0/0	0/0	0	6
Willie Green	1	0	1	0/0	0/0	0	6
Broncos	62	26	32	23/27	58/58	0	501
Opponents	32	8	28	28	14/20	0	305

SCORING BY PERIODS

	1	2	3	4	OT	Pts.
Broncos	144	156	64	137	0	501
Opponent	54	87	58	110	0	309

	Denver	Opp.
Total First Downs	347	283
Rushing	135	80
Passing	186	183
Penalty	26	20
3rd Down: Made/Att	90/207	88/225
3rd Down Pct.	43.5	39.1
4th Down: Made/Att	4/10	10/19
4th Down Pct.	40.0	52.6
Possession Avg.	32:08	27:52
Total Net Yards	6092	4935
Avg. Per Game	380.8	308.4
Avg. Per Play	5.9	4.9
Net Yards Rushing	2468	1287
Avg. Per Game	154.3	80.4
Avg. Per Attempt	4.7	3.6
Total Rushes	525	356
Net Yards Passing	3624	3648
Avg. Per Game	226.5	228.0
Avg. Per Play	7.02	5.67
Sacked/Yards Lost	25/184	47/335
Gross Yards	3808	3983
Att./Completions	491/290	596/345
Completion Pct.	59.1	57.9
Had Intercepted	14	19
Punts/Average	67/46.2	88/42.4
Penalties/Yards	115/1023	113/865
Fumbles/Ball Lost	17/6	28/11
Touchdowns	62	38
Rushing	26	8
Passing	32	28
Misc	4	2

SCORING

	Tot. TD	Rush	Rec.	FG	PAT	S	Pts.
Terrell Davis	23	21	2	0/0	0/0	0	138
Jason Elam	0	0	0	23/27	58/58	0	127
Ed McCaffrey	10	0	10	0/0	0/0	0	62
Shannon Sharpe	10	0	10	0/0	0/0	0	60
Rod Smith	7	0	6	0/0	0/0	0	42
Howard Griffith	3	0	3	0/0	0/0	0	18
Vaughn Hebron	2	1	0	0/0	0/0	0	12
Derek Loville	2	2	0	0/0	0/0	0	12
Bubby Brister	1	1	0	0/0	0/0	0	6
Ray Crockett	1	0	0	0/0	0/0	0	6
John Elway	1	1	0	0/0	0/0	0	6
Darrien Gordon	1	0	0	0/0	0/0	0	6
Willie Green	1	0	1	0/0	0/0	0	6
Broncos	62	26	32	23/27	58/58	0	501
Opponents	32	8	28	28	14/20	0	305

PASSING

	Att.	Cmp.	Yds.	Cmp%	Yds./Att.	TD	TD%	Int.	Int%	Long	Sack/Lost	Rating
John Elway	356	210	2806	59.0	7.88	22	6.2	10	2.8	58	18/135	93.0
Bubby Brister	131	78	986	59.5	7.53	10	7.6	3	2.3	48	7/49	99.0
Rod Smith	1	1	14	100.0	14.00	0	0.0	0	0.0	14	0/0	118.8
Brian Griese	3	1	2	33.3	0.67	0	0.0	1	33.3	2	0/0	2.8

RUSHING

	No.	Yds.	Avg.	Long	TD
Terrell Davis	392	2008	5.1	70	21
Derek Loville	53	161	3.0	12	2
Bubby Brister	19	102	5.4	38t	1
John Elway	37	94	2.5	16	1
Rod Smith	6	63	10.5	37	0
Vaughn Hebron	9	31	3.4	8	1
Howard Griffith	4	13	3.3	16	0
Tom Rouen	1	0	0.0	0	0
Brian Griese	4	-4	-1.0	0	0

RECEIVING

	No.	Yds.	Avg.	Long	TD
Rod Smith	86	1222	14.2	58	6
Ed McCaffrey	64	1053	16.5	48	10
Shannon Sharpe	64	768	12.0	38t	10
Terrell Davis	25	217	8.7	35	2
Willie Green	16	194	12.1	50	1
Howard Griffith	15	97	6.5	15	3
Dwayne Carswell	4	51	12.8	15	0
Marcus Nash	4	76	19.0	31	0
Byron Chamberlain	3	35	11.7	16	0
Detron Smith	3	24	8.0	16	0
Vaughn Hebron	2	5	2.5	3	0
Derek Loville	2	29	14.5	17	0
Justin Armour	1	23	23.0	23	0
John Elway	1	14	14.0	14	0

INDIVIDUAL DEFENSE

	Tackles	Solo	Asst.	Sacks	Fum. Rec.
John Mobley	117	98	19	1.0	1
Glenn Cadrez	78	60	18	4.0	0
Bill Romanowski	70	55	15	7.5	3
Darrien Gordon	63	57	6	0.0	1
Steve Atwater	55	43	12	0.0	0
Ray Crockett	51	46	5	0.5	0
Maa Tanuvasa	44	33	11	8.5	2
Darrius Johnson	43	38	5	1.0	0
Trevor Pryce	43	30	13	8.5	0
Tyrone Braxton	39	33	6	0.0	0
Eric Brown	38	29	9	0.0	1
Keith Traylor	32	24	8	2.0	1
Keith Burns	27	17	10	0.0	1
Neil Smith	26	20	6	4.0	0
Tory James	23	18	5	0.0	1
Marvin Washington	23	14	9	2.0	0
Harald Hasselbach	21	19	2	3.0	0
George Coghill	16	15	1	0.0	0
Anthony Lynn	16	10	6	0.0	0
Tito Paul	15	11	4	0.0	1
Detron Smith	15	11	4	0.0	0
Alfred Williams	13	10	3	3.0	0
Derek Loville	12	11	1	0.0	0
Dwayne Carswell	10	6	4	0.0	0
Seth Joyner	7	5	2	0.0	0
Byron Chamberlain	6	3	3	0.0	0
Mike Lodish	6	5	1	2.0	0
Shannon Sharpe	3	3	0	0.0	0
Ed McCaffrey	2	2	0	0.0	0
Nate Wayne	2	2	0	0.0	0
Bubby Brister	1	1	0	0.0	1
Jason Elam	1	1	0	0.0	0
Tony Jones	1	1	0	0.0	0
Tom Nalen	1	1	0	0.0	0
Tom Rouen	1	1	0	0.0	0
Mark Schlereth	1	1	0	0.0	0
Rod Smith	1	1	0	0.0	2
Broncos	923	735	188	47.0	15
Opponents	990	781	209	25.0	23

INTERCEPTIONS

	No.	Yds.	Avg.	Long	TD
Darrien Gordon	4	125	31.3	55t	1
Ray Crockett	3	105	35.0	80t	1
Glenn Cadrez	2	11	5.5	6	0
Darrius Johnson	2	79	39.5	45	0
Bill Romanowski	2	22	11.0	18	0
Steve Atwater	1	4	4.0	4	0
Tyrone Braxton	1	72	72.0	72	0
George Coghill	1	20	20.0	20	0
John Mobley	1	-2	-2.0	-2	0
Trevor Pryce	1	1	1.0	1	0
Neil Smith	1	2	2.0	2	0
Broncos	19	439	23.1	80t	2
Opponents	14	270	19.3	94t	2

FIELD GOALS

	1-19	20-29	30-39	40-49	50+
Jason Elam	0/0	3/3	13/14	4/6	3/4
Broncos	0/0	3/3	13/14	4/6	3/4
Opponents	0/0	0/0	0/0	0/0	0/0

PUNTING

	No.	Avg.	Net	T'back	In20	Long
Tom Rouen	66	46.9	37.6	10	14	76
Broncos	66	46.9	37.6	10	14	76
Opponents	87	42.9	36.1	8	22	69

KICKOFF RETURNS

	No.	Yds.	Avg.	Long	TD
Vaughn Hebron	46	1216	26.4	95t	1
Derek Loville	6	105	17.5	25	0
Detron Smith	3	51	17.0	21	0
Keith Burns	2	17	8.5	17	0
Maa Tanuvasa	1	13	13.0	13	0
Broncos	58	1402	24.2	95t	1
Opponents	89	2006	22.5	91	0

PUNT RETURNS

	Ret.	FC	Yds.	Avg.	Long	TD
Darrien Gordon	34	6	379	11.1	44	0
George Coghill	3	2	22	7.3	10	0
Tito Paul	1	0	0	0.0	0	0
Broncos	38	8	401	10.6	44	0
Opponents	43	2	381	8.9	39	0

Playoff Statistics

SCORING STATS

	Tot. TD	Rush	Rec.	FG	PAT	S	Pts
Jason Elam	0	0	0	4/4	7/7	0	19
Terrell Davis	3	3	0	0/0	0/0	0	18
Howard Griffith	1	0	1	0/0	0/0	0	6
Derek Loville	1	1	0	0/0	0/0	0	6
Neil Smith	1	0	0	0/0	0/0	0	6
Rod Smith	1	0	1	0/0	0/0	0	6
Broncos	7	4	2	4/4	7/7	0	61
Opponents	1	1	0	0	2/3	0	13

SCORING BY PERIODS

	1	2	3	4	OT	Pts.
Broncos	14	7	23	17	0	61
Opponent	0	6	7	0	0	13

RUSHING

	No.	Yds.	Avg.	Long	TD
Terrell Davis	53	366	6.9	62	3
Derek Loville	10	41	4.1	11t	1
John Elway	6	32	5.3	11	0
Bubby Brister	6	-2	-0.3	2	0
Tom Rouen	1	-9	-9.0	-9	0

TEAM STATS

	Denver	Opp.
Total First Downs	38	32
Rushing	21	2
Passing	16	28
Penalty	1	2
3rd Down: Made/Att	9/30	5/22
3rd Down Pct.	30.0	22.7
4th Down: Made/Att	3/7	2/3
4th Down Pct.	42.9	66.7
Possession Avg.	32:42	27:18
Total Net Yards	755	622
Avg. Per Game	377.5	311.0
Avg. Per Play	5.5	5.4
Net Yards Rushing	428	28
Avg. Per Game	214.0	14.0
Avg. Per Attempt	5.6	1.1
Total Rushes	76	26
Net Yards Passing	327	594
Avg. Per Game	163.5	297.0
Avg. Per Play	5.36	6.6
Sacked/Yards Lost	4/28	1/5
Gross Yards	355	599
Att./Completions	57/27	89/57
Completion Pct.	47.4	64.0
Had Intercepted	0	4
Punts/Average	10/41.4	12/46.9
Penalties/Yards	11/88	16/106
Fumbles/Ball Lost	2/0	5/5
Touchdowns	7	1
Rushing	4	1
Passing	2	0
Misc	1	0

RECEIVING

	No.	Yds.	Avg.	Long	TD
Shannon Sharpe	7	52	7.4	10	0
Rod Smith	7	108	15.4	28t	1
Ed McCaffrey	6	118	19.7	47	0
Byron Chamberlain	2	26	13.0	16	0
Terrell Davis	2	19	9.5	12	0
Howard Griffith	2	25	12.5	14	1
Dwayne Carswell	1	7	7.0	7	0

FIELD GOALS

	1-19	20-29	30-39	40-49	50+
Jason Elam	0/0	0/0	0/0	1/1	1/1
Broncos	0/0	0/0	0/0	1/1	1/1
Opponents	0/0	0/0	0/0	0/0	0/0

PUNTING

	No.	Avg.	Net	T'back	In20	Long	B
Tom Rouen	9	46.0	34.0	1	3	59	1
Broncos	9	46.0	34.0	1	3	59	1
Opponents	12	46.9	39.2	0	5	56	0

KICKOFF RETURNS

	No.	Yds.	Avg.	Long	TD
Vaughn Hebron	2	47	23.5	28	0
Broncos	2	47	23.5	28	0
Opponents	10	167	16.7	35	0

PUNT RETURNS

	Ret.	FC	Yds.	Avg.	Long	TD
Darrien Gordon	7	1	93	13.3	36	0
Broncos	7	1	93	13.3	36	0
Opponents	4	0	54	13.5	33	0

INDIVIDUAL DEFENSE

	Tackles	Solo	Asst.	Sacks	Fum. Rec.
Bill Romanowski	16	10	6	0.0	1
Darrius Johnson	13	9	4	0.0	0
Ray Crockett	12	8	4	0.0	0
John Mobley	11	9	2	0.0	1
Steve Atwater	8	5	3	0.0	0
Tyrone Braxton	8	7	1	0.0	1
Darrien Gordon	6	3	3	0.0	0
Glenn Cadrez	5	3	2	0.0	0
Keith Burns	4	2	2	0.0	1
Alfred Williams	4	3	1	0.0	0
Harald Hasselbach	3	0	3	0.0	0
Tito Paul	3	2	1	0.0	0
Trevor Pryce	3	1	2	0.0	0
Keith Traylor	3	2	1	0.0	0
Marvin Washington	3	3	0	1.0	0
Tory James	2	2	0	0.0	0
Detron Smith	2	0	2	0.0	0
Maa Tanuvasa	2	1	1	0.0	0
Dwayne Carswell	1	1	0	0.0	0
George Coghill	1	1	0	0.0	0
Derek Loville	1	1	0	0.0	0
Anthony Lynn	1	1	0	0.0	0
Tom Rouen	1	1	0	0.0	1
Broncos	113	75	38	1.0	5
Opponents	128	92	36	4.0	0

INTERCEPTIONS

	No.	Yds.	Avg.	Long	TD
Darrien Gordon	2	48	24.0	30	0
Darrius Johnson	1	48	48.0	48	0
Bill Romanowski	1	0	0.0	0	0
Broncos	4	96	24.0	48	0
Opponents	0	0	–	0	0

PASSING

	Att.	Cmp.	Yds.	Cmp%	Yds./Att.	TD	TD%	Int.	Int%	Long	Sack/Lost	Rating
John Elway	57	27	355	47.4	6.23	2	3.5	0	0.0	47	4/28	79.2

‘This one’s for

A look back at the Broncos’ first Super Bowl championship

By Clay Latimer

When the Denver Broncos returned home from their stirring victory in Super Bowl XXXII, 650,000 euphoric fans jammed downtown streets and the Civic Center to greet their happy warriors.

Some fans danced in the streets, some climbed onto roofs for the big picture, some pranced around with orange wigs, and some wept.

“I never thought this day would come,” a middle-aged fan said.

He had plenty of company. Before their 31-24 win over Green Bay, the Broncos were 0-4 in the Ultimate Game, including a 55-10 loss to Green Bay in XXIV, the most one-sided defeat in Super Bowl history.

“Now the suffering is over,” a woman said.

Added John Elway; “I can’t express it in words. I can’t believe it.”

Few could, because at several points during the season, it appeared Elway and Co. wouldn’t even get a shot at Super Bowl redemption:

John'

During a pre-season game in Mexico City, Elway stumbled off the field, his right arm swollen like a melon. "I thought it was over," said the 15-year veteran, whose biceps tendon had detached from his shoulder. No quarterback of note has ever thrown a pass without a biceps tendon. But eight days later Elway's ball had just as much zip as ever, and the Broncos had averted their first crisis.

• In Week 11, the Broncos began a late-season collapse when Kansas City's Pete Stoyanovich kicked a 54-yard field goal as time wound down for a 24-22 win.
• Three weeks later, the Pittsburgh Steelers bombed the Broncos 35-24 at Three Rivers Stadium, leaving Elway dismayed. "I get a little upset at the fact that it seems like every time we've been asked to answer the bell in big games, especially the last couple years, we haven't answered the bell," he said.
• The Broncos stumbled again the following week, losing to San Francisco 34-17 during a Monday Night Game in which Terrell Davis was forced to the sideline with a mild shoulder separation and Bill Romanowski was caught spitting in the face of 49ers wide receiver J.J. Stokes. Romanowski apologized profusely, and accepted without a complaint a $7,500 NFL fine. But some of his teammates had bitter feelings. Willie Green said the NFL was racist for not fining Romanowski more, and that a black player would've paid a higher price.

The last-season collapse had transformed Denver into a wild-card team, and only one wild-card team, the Oakland Raiders, had ever won a Super Bowl.

But the Revenge Tour soon was underway. A week later, the Broncos beat Jacksonville – the team that had knocked them out of post-season play the year before – 42-17 at Mile High Stadium.

In the next two weeks, the Broncos beat Kansas City 14-10 at Arrowhead Stadium and the Steelers 24-21 in the AFC Championship Game at Three Rivers Stadium.

As the Broncos and Green Bay Packers began making preparations for Super Bowl XXXII, it became clear that Elway was the people's choice, 15 years after he and Dan Marino, Jim Kelly and the Great Class of 1983 bounded into the NFL, the world at their feet.

Even Brett Favre was an Elway fan.

"If I wasn't playing against him, I'd be pulling for him," Favre said.

Added Elway: "Maybe people feel bad for the old guy."

Following the opening kickoff of Super Bowl XXXII, the Packers, 13.5 point favorites, marched for a TD. But the Broncos responded with a 12-play scoring drive of their own, with Davis finishing things off with a 1-yard run.

On the Packers' second possession, Tyrone Braxton picked off a Favre pass, setting up Elway and Co. on Green Bay's 45. Once again, the Broncos dominated the line of scrimmage, and Elway scored on a 1-yard run, which lifted Denver to a 14-7 lead. Elway then hurried to the sideline to check on Davis, who was down with a migraine.

"I couldn't see, and when that happens, it's a sign a migraine is coming," Davis said.

Before Davis left the game, the Broncos had 94 yards of offense; after that, 14.

But a few minutes later, Steve Atwater sacked Favre, forcing a fumble that defensive end Neil Smith recovered at the Green Bay 33. Four plays later, Jason Elam kicked a 51-yard field goal to increase Denver's lead to 17-7. In the fading minutes of the first half, however, the Packers drove 95 yards for a TD, with Favre throwing a 6-yard scoring pass to tight end Mark Chmura with 12 seconds left. That cut Denver's lead to 17-14.

The Broncos hadn't scored in the third quarter in three playoff wins, and with Davis' status uncertain, the pressure was clearly on Elway, who had thrown for 27 yards in the first half, compared to Favre's 127.

The Broncos' biggest fear was a turnover, which could give the Packers a short field. Sure enough, Davis fumbled on the first play of the second half, giving the Packers the ball on Denver's 26.

But Denver's D limited Green Bay to a 29-yard Ryan Longwell field goal that tied the score 17-17.

On their third possession of the third quarter, the Broncos began one of their most dramatic scoring drives of the long season at the 8. Elway hit wideout Ed McCaffrey twice for combined gains of 45 yards, and Davis resumed his groundbreaking ways.

But Elway came up with the biggest play. On third-and-12, he dropped back to pass, saw Reggie White rushing at him from his left end spot, stepped up in the pocket, saw an opening, and went for it.

First he dodged a tackle, knowing he had to get to the 5 for a first down, to avoid settling for a field goal. Then, as three defenders converged, Elway launched himself into a headlong dive for the chalk line. A mid-air collision flipped him around, but the 37-year-old QB crash landed in first-down territory. Elway's willingness to sacrifice his body for a victory galvanized his teammates. "From that point on, I knew we had it," linebacker John Mobley said.

Shortly after Elway's play, Davis scored on a 1-yard run and Denver led 24-17. Later in the final quarter, after the Packers tied the score 24-24 on a 13-yard scoring pass from Favre to Antonio Freeman, the Broncos mounted the game-winning scoring drive, with Davis capping it off with a 1-yard run. Davis, almost felled by a migraine in the first half, earned the MVP trophy for his second-half performance. But Elway was the real hero.

After accepting the Super Bowl trophy, Denver owner Pat Bowlen said, "This one's for John." •